HAUNTED ONTARIO

HAUNTED ONTARIO

~ SECOND EDITION ~

Ghostly Inns, Hotels, and Other Eerie Places

TERRY BOYLE

DUNDURN
TORONTO

Editor: Laura Harris
Design: Courtney Horner
Printer: Webcom

Library and Archives Canada Cataloguing in Publication

Boyle, Terry
    Haunted Ontario : ghostly inns, hotels, and other eerie places / Terry Boyle. -- 2nd ed.

Includes index.
Issued also in electronic formats.
ISBN 978-1-4597-0741-2

    1. Haunted places--Ontario. 2. Haunted hotels--Ontario.
I. Title.

BF1472.C3B69 2013   133.109713   C2012-904619-1

1   2   3   4   5   17   16   15   14   13

We acknowledge the support of the **Canada Council for the Arts** and the **Ontario Arts Council** for our publishing program. We also acknowledge the financial support of the **Government of Canada** through the **Canada Book Fund** and **Livres Canada Books**, and the **Government of Ontario** through the **Ontario Book Publishing Tax Credit** and the **Ontario Media Development Corporation**.

Care has been taken to trace the ownership of copyright material used in this book. The author and the publisher welcome any information enabling them to rectify any references or credits in subsequent editions.

J. Kirk Howard, President

Printed and bound in Canada.

Visit us at
Dundurn.com
Definingcanada.ca
@dundurnpress
Facebook.com/dundurnpress

Dundurn	Gazelle Book Services Limited	Dundurn
3 Church Street, Suite 500	White Cross Mills	2250 Military Road
Toronto, Ontario, Canada	High Town, Lancaster, England	Tonawanda, NY
M5E 1M2	LA1 4XS	U.S.A. 14150

Dedicated to Allana, and Bob Sutton, a man of great spirit

Contents

Introduction

As a young child I would wait anxiously for sleep. Bed never seemed a particular secure place. It was dark; I felt alone and vulnerable in the night. The subtle play of shadows on the walls and the flowing, bulky curtains danced the waltz of the unknown. The night closed the door to sight and light. There was no comfort, no warmth; it was very still. It would happen then.

From the depths of mystery a vision would begin. Spiralling, spiralling, the image would draw closer ever brighter and clearer like a shooting star at night.

My eyes, forced to open, were pierced by light. Filled with terror, I would shake and scream aloud from the suffocating feeling in my room. As quickly as it occurred, it disappeared. Fear had slammed the door.

These visitations continued throughout my childhood. At first my screams of panic brought my mother to the room where she offered comfort to me and encouraged me to go back to sleep. Her warmth and kindness brought the light back, and yet I knew "it" lurked there still.

The frequency of visitations enabled me to understand how to bring them forth at will. If I welcomed the experience without fear and allowed it to spiral freely, I knew then, in my heart, that something very unique and special would take place — something very different. Unfortunately, it never became clearer than a blur because it happened very fast and as I grew it happened less frequently.

What was it? To see it clearly never seemed to be the important thing but I did know that it was real!

Many children have this kind of experience, perhaps only later dismissed or forgotten. Others may have had similar experiences that were, unfortunately, unexplained and undeveloped. A child that has a conversation with an imaginary friend may be having a visionary experience. We adults may tell our children that their friend is imaginary, but perhaps the child does see a spirit. It may be very real to them. Do we disregard a child's experience because we cannot see it? This is the time of life to clarify those experiences and assist in the development of the gift of spirit connection as something very real and very special.

So, here I am once again exploring this unknown world. At last I am communicating with people whose experiences have somehow shaped their lives in a different way. For want of another way to phrase it, this is a book about hauntings.

Many people are keen to understand this phenomenal world. How about you? I believe we often refrain from admitting it publicly in fear, but deep in the depths of one's consciousness lives a belief about spirits. We just need some form of permission or acceptance from someone. You see, fear calls too many shots. How many people are afraid to walk downstairs into a basement by themselves? Are you afraid to be left at home alone overnight? Do you leave a light on at night after retiring to bed? How do you feel when the power goes out and you are left in the darkness? Will you stay alone in a house that is reputed to have a ghost?

Fear of the unknown. What the rational mind cannot comprehend does not exist. There is a need to open ourselves to more than our sense-body awareness, to experience dimensions of awareness that are there, and already available to some. All we need to do is believe.

What keeps spirits active in this dimension? What is a ghost? This is what the experts have to say. Reverend William Rauscher in his book *The Spiritual Frontier*, states, "The question 'What is a ghost?' is rather like asking; 'What's an animal?' Animals come in all shapes and sizes, as mammals, birds, fish and reptiles and range in appearance from the cuddlesome calf or bear cub to the fearsome crocodile or boa constrictor. Ghosts are similarly diverse."

The *Random House Dictionary* defines a ghost as "the soul of a dead person, a disembodied spirit imagined usually as a vague, shadowy or evanescent form, as wandering among or haunting living persons."

A recent survey in Britain showed that over half the population believed in psychic phenomena and that 44 percent of people believed in ghosts. Of these, one in seven claimed to have seen a ghost or been haunted by one. The figures in the United States are even higher; similar studies revealed that 57 percent of the adult population believed in the phenomenon. One might conclude, to deny ghosts exist is to ignore the millions of ordinary witnesses to them.

So what happens when a person dies? Eddie Burk and Gillian Cribbs, in their book entitled *Ghosthunter*, addressed this question. Mr. Burk believes that in the dying moments consciousness begins to drift to a higher level of existence, and often relatives and loved ones will appear. Then the person passes out of the physical body and into the "etheric body." The etheric body is a halfway house between the physical and spiritual bodies: when you die your consciousness moves out of the physical body and operates through the etheric body. If you remain in the etheric body for too long, your consciousness begins to cloud; this is why ghosts have no idea how long they have been trapped — in the etheric body there is no difference between a day and a hundred years. He also believed that up to one in five hundred people remain back in this etheric place after death.

Ms. Elizabeth P. Hoffman, author of *In Search of Ghosts: Haunted Places in Delaware Valley*, defines ghosts as the spirits of people, places, creatures, or objects. She says a place is haunted if a spirit is felt, heard, sensed, seen, or smelled. She also maintains that the temperature may drop or the atmosphere will feel cool and damp when a spirit is near.

A ghost may be present when something physical — a picture, a book, a dish moves without a natural cause such as a vibration or a slammed door.

A hundred years ago Mrs. Eleanor Sidgwick of the Society for Psychical Research analyzed more than 300 case histories and observed that a ghost is usually seen upon looking around the room, or comes in a door, or forms gradually out of a cloud. It rarely simply pops into place. It can disappear suddenly, however, if the viewer looks away or blinks. The form can also vanish slowly as if in a cloud. Frequently it will go through a door, open or closed, or it will move to another room where it cannot be found.

Many ordinary families who find out their home is haunted first experience fear. Others simply accept the fact that someone or something is sharing their humble abode. I have known some people to open their home up to the public and share their ghost story. Such was the case with an old historic estate, named "the Hermitage" in South Carolina.

I first became acquainted with the Hermitage in 1975, when I was researching historical sketches of places on the Waccamaw Neck of South Carolina, United States. Stories of ghosts that inhabit old residences in South Carolina are not unusual. The Hermitage, at the time, was a good example of a house with an appealing combination of the historic and the mysterious. After all it is a house with a benign ghost.

Dr. Allard Belin Flagg built the Hermitage on a point of land surrounded on three sides by tidal marshes in Murrells Inlet. He placed his home within a grove of live oaks, which, at the time (1849), were undoubtedly 100 years old. Some say the land was given to Flagg's mother by her brother on the condition that the doctor build there. The land might well have been a wedding gift for he was married the following year. Clarke A. Wilcox, the owner at the time, shared this about the estate: "The property contained 937 acres. On the north, a bank thrown up by slaves separated it from Sunnyside plantation, home of J. Motte Alston. On the south, Dr. James Grant owned the land west of the present King's Highway. One hundred acres at the eastern end of the south line was the property of the Rev. James L. Belin, who left the tract to the Methodist Church."

For decades the Hermitage was isolated. Mr. Wilcox adds, "When I was a boy, Sunnyside and the Belin property were our closest neighbours and we had to go through the field about half a mile to reach the winding one-way road to either of these places."

No description of the Hermitage would be complete without the legend of lovely Alice Belin Flagg, the 16-year-old sister of the doctor. Engaged to a man in the turpentine industry and aware of her brother's disapproval, she wore her ring on a ribbon around her neck and concealed it inside her blouse when she was at home on vacation from finishing school in Charleston. Her mother, fleeing from the dreaded malaria season, was in the mountains. At home the doctor was tending his patients and operating the farm. Following her happy debut at the spring ball in Charleston, Alice was suddenly stricken with a fever that was prevalent in the area. The school authorities sent for Dr. Flagg, who was experienced in treating fevers. After equipping the family carriage with articles for Alice's comfort, he set out with a servant over miserable roads with five rivers to ford — a four-day trip one way.

Mr. Wilcox relates this portion of the story: "Upon examining his delirious sister when they arrived home, he found the ring. In great anger he removed it and threw it into the creek. Thinking she had lost it, Alice begged everyone who came into her sickroom to find the ring — her most cherished possession. Sensing her distress, a cousin went to Georgetown and bought a ring. When he pressed it into her hand, she threw it on the floor and insisted that they find her ring."

Alice died prior to her mother's return from the mountains, and was buried temporarily in the yard. When her mother returned, Alice's body was moved to the family plot at All-Saints Episcopal Church on the river opposite Pawley's Island. Among the imposing stones raised in memory of the other Flaggs, a flat marble slab, upon which is engraved the single word, "Alice," marks her grave. The conjecture of an older resident, "Perhaps she was so beloved that is all that was needed," fails to dissipate an observer's feeling of sadness. Often a vase of flowers appears on her grave. The donors are unknown. Young people often walk around the site 13 times backward, lie on the grave and, as they say, "talk to her spirit." It is said that if a young girl sets her ring on the grave and runs round the grave nine times with her eyes closed, she will find, upon opening them, that her ring has disappeared.

Still searching for her ring, Alice visits her old room in the Hermitage. The Wilcox's say that there is an undeniable feeling of her presence, more real than a visual appearance and far more impressive. They even left Alice's room untouched, appearing as it did the night she passed away. At one time visitors were allowed to tour the house and spend some time in Alice's room.

A few years ago the Hermitage property was sold and the house moved down the street. It is now a private residence.

Some people still say Alice returns on moonlit nights when the shadows of the restless moss, the eerie cry of the whippoorwill, and the distant roar of the ocean put the expectant one in the mood. At such times the beauteous Alice becomes real to even the most skeptical beholder.

The fact that ghosts haunt particular places could be in some way linked to a strong emotion or attachment to some item, such as Alice of the Hermitage, who is still looking for her engagement ring. Many spirits are so attached to personal items and familiar surroundings that they refuse to cross over to the other side. Instead, they remain in their homes.

A few years ago I resided in a grand century-old home that was still inhabited by the previous owners. They had never crossed over to the other side. Two family members had been seen on numerous occasions in the house, sitting on the front veranda and standing at the head of the stairs. I still remember the first night I spent here. I slept on the second floor of the building in the room to the right of the hall in the front part of the house.

That very night I had a dream — or was it a dream? I recall watching a procession of people carrying a casket along the second floor hall and down the central staircase. One thing that stood out in this image was a man following behind, who was dragging his leg. That was it. I awoke to brilliant rays of light beaming in my bedroom window. Was it just a dream? No.

Over morning coffee I shared this unusual dream. My friend replied, "The brother of the deceased was known to have a bad leg."

What I had witnessed truly happened years before I was even born. Everything in my dream was as it had occurred. Somehow I had connected with the past.

A part of my childhood feels finally fulfilled to have travelled to these many diverse locations with the specific intention to feel, see, hear, smell, or otherwise experience the spirit activity to be found there. The hauntings have in no way been sensationalized and in many cases the accounts have actually been condensed. What we have here are personal reports of experiences that are often quite difficult to articulate.

I trust this book will speak to you if you have had childhood experiences that were unexplained by ordinary life, and if you believe but have had no chance to experience. One must believe the many folks who have shared their experiences with humour and candour. They have also opened their doors and their hearts to me; for that I am extremely grateful. For them, and many who will visit them, the spirit world does indeed exist in their surroundings every day.

Terry Boyle
Burk's Falls
February 2012

The Swastika Hotel

~ Bala (now the Bala Bay Inn) ~

THE YEAR IS 1910 AND IT IS DINNERTIME. WOMEN DRESSED IN LONG gowns with Gibson hairdos and gentlemen in black evening suits are escorted to the dining room. The tables are set; the service is simple, but elegant and tasteful. Outside, the sun is glistening on the waters of Lake Muskoka. Welcome to the Swastika Hotel in Bala, Ontario.

This elaborate hotel, built on land deeded to the owner on the condition that alcohol would never be sold on the property, is haunted today. Did a spirit refuse to leave? Perhaps it's about the broken promise concerning the sale of alcohol; perhaps it's about attachment to a grand hotel, too much to leave behind. Whatever the reasons, the Bala Bay Inn, as it is known today, remains one of the most intriguing haunted sites in Ontario.

The story of the inn begins in 1882 when Ephraim Browning Sutton and his wife Rose set sail from England after three of their children died as a result of unsanitary government vaccination programs. Upon landing, Ephraim said to his wife, "If only Clara could have seen this."

The general store E.B. Sutton built on land purchased from the temperance-minded Thomas Burgess.

Swastika Hotel, 1921

Clara had died in her tenth year from vaccination complications. Two younger children died in the same way.

Mr. Sutton was born in Leeds, England, in 1854. He worked in the office of a publishing firm, Rivington and Sons. Involvement in the literary world was familiar to the family, since his cousin was the well-known poet, Robert Browning. Sometime later Sutton entered railway life, in the service of the Midland and Great Western Railways, until he moved to Canada. At the age of 18, Sutton married his second cousin, Rose Anne Grey, who was ten years his senior, and had one daughter from an earlier marriage.

In 1882 they chose to settle on the west side of Lake Muskoka. At the time the district appeared to be quite hostile to settlers arriving from England. There was bush to clear, harsh winters, and if that wasn't enough, there were blackflies and mosquitoes. Nevertheless, the Suttons, pioneers at heart, cleared their own land in Medora Township, known today as Bannockburn.

The Suttons had two objectives in mind for their 50-acre property. Their first aim was to clear the land to farm and support themselves; their second aim was to develop a summer resort, a magnificent two-storey wooden structure with a sit-out verandah and a gable that overlooked Lake Muskoka. They hoped that such a structure and setting would attract American tourists. The name Camp Sutton was, in fact, given to the establishment by U.S. Civil War veterans who left the Solid Comfort Club of Beaumaris in search of better fishing.

It wasn't long before Canadian newspapers became aware of E.B. Sutton. He was never afraid to voice his opinions, and on September 15, 1890, was reported to have lectured his neighbours on their small-minded tendency to resist new ideas in Muskoka. "It is a notable fact that whenever a notion is put forward of great and lasting utility to the public, it is confronted with an array of opposition," he said. For three decades he wrote for the *Orillia Times*. His pen name was "The Muskoka Bard," and he often lectured in his columns about how farmers should not build barns on slopes that lead down to water, and he warned tourists not to use the lakes for bathing. His main aim was to preserve the Muskoka lakes for future generations. He may still have a message for us.

Early advertising for the Swastika Hotel, billed as "Canada's Popular Summer Resort," 1915.

In January 1884 the Suttons were blessed with the arrival of a son, Frederick. On October 14, 1898, E.B. Sutton purchased another piece of property in Bala from Thomas Burgess, the founder of the community, and there he constructed a general store. Burgess was a Scot by birth, a Presbyterian and a Grit. When Burgess sold the land to E.B. he stipulated the following in the deed of land: "His heirs, executors ... or any person or persons ... will not at any time hereafter use or permit to be used any building or erection of any kind now built ... upon the said lands for the sale, barter or disposal of any spirituous or fermented or intoxicating liquors of any kind whatever."

By this time, tourists and sportsmen had discovered the beauties of this area and were creating a demand for accommodation. Lamb from the area became so famous for its exceptional flavour that posh hotels and restaurants in New York City started to include "Muskoka Lamb" on their menus.

The first hotel in Bala was the Clifton House, the second the Bala Falls Hotel, and the third, the Swastika — Muskoka's first brick hotel, a summer hotel, owned and operated by E.B. Sutton. The swastika was an ancient symbol for well-being and benediction in the form of a Greek cross, each arm bent at a right angle. In 1910, E.B. and his son, Fred,

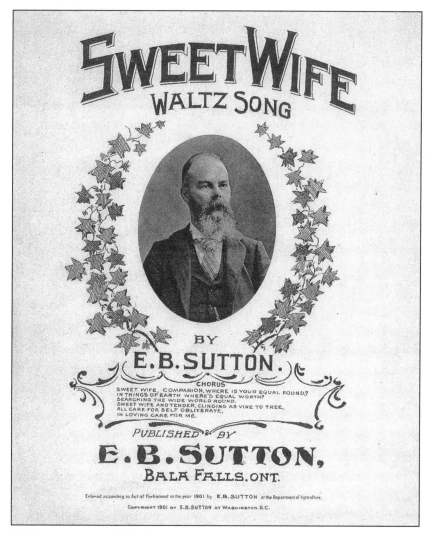

E.B. Sutton was a published composer.

built the three-storey hotel in the Muskokas on a piece of land across from their mercantile business. He had three swastikas engraved in the brick exterior of the building. The property itself, facing Lake Muskoka, was a picturesque site. The land consisted of 23 acres and included riding trails for hotel guests. The train station was a short walk or buggyride away. E.B., quite aware of his agreement with Burgess in 1899, honoured the land deal by not allowing any alcohol to be served in his hotel. This agreement may be the reason the hotel later became haunted.

Guests enjoying amenities at the swastika, date unknown.

As the hotel neared completion, the Suttons began to prepare for a grand celebration, the likes of which Bala had never seen before. In his column E.B. noted, "Even the old folks who are supposed to take no stock in such frivolities were seen wandering home after daylight. Everything went as merry as a marriage bell. The music was supplied by five players and relays for the piano, and consisted of mandolin, guitar, violin and snare drum, an orchestra as unique as their music was fine. The Minett steam launch brought a contingent from Port Carling, while another craft brought the musicians from Bracebridge. There was just enough wax, and just enough spring from the floor, and the number of feet might be 30 score. Oh! What a time we had."

Bala was entering the age of tourism, when families arrived for a week or more during the summer. Leisure time meant tennis, boating, fishing, horseback riding, or simply strolling along the shore of Lake Muskoka. Steamer service provided tourists with the opportunity to visit other parts of the Muskoka Lakes. It was an age of elegant relaxation.

Lillian Sutton (left) wearing a dress made from War Bonds.

In 1907 Rose and Ephraim left for a trip to England. During their stay E.B. visited British doctors who confirmed what he already suspected. He was diagnosed with what was then called "hardening of the arteries," a condition which eventually would lead to his death.

In 1914, a summer holiday visitor to Bala became acquainted with Fred Sutton, the tall, dashing, young son of E.B., who operated the hotel with his father. All the evidence indicates that the Sutton family, who had lost their own daughters, were soon attached to this vivacious 20-year-old, Lillian Holden, who loved to dance and sing. E.B., a composer in

Lillian Holden before she became Mrs. Fred Sutton.

his own right (including seven published tunes) was charmed by her. He praised her as "the best of all jewels — a true woman" and presented her with a three-quarter size Stradivarius violin.

By now E.B. was using a cane, crippled with arthritis, and in need of increasing care from his son and his wife.

Lillian Holden and two unidentified friends, all are wearing matching outfits.

Shortly before Thanksgiving in 1916, Lillian and Fred announced their engagement. Their happiness was cut short on Thanksgiving weekend when Rose suffered a stroke while doing the family laundry. She staggered back to their living quarters and died 15 minutes later in E.B.'s arms. Fred and Lillian had little choice but to delay their wedding date to the following January.

Mrs. E.B. Sutton, probably around the turn of the twentieth century.

Lillian recalled a remarkable event in mid-August 1917, when she entered room 319, E.B.'s quarters. She discovered the sad shadow of a once-great and energetic man with tears streaming down his face. "I'm sorry," he said. "I've just been wondering whether I'll ever see my Rose again."

"I told him that of course he would," recalled Lillian. "That didn't seem to satisfy him because he said people just went into a deep sleep at death. So, trying to cheer him up, I said that if I died before he did I'd come back and give three loud knocks as a signal that I was on the other side. He seemed to perk up at that thought and said that he'd make the same promise to me."

A few weeks later Ephraim Sutton passed away quietly in his sleep. The family laid his body in state in what was the dining room on the ground floor of the hotel, just beyond the main foyer. The first sign of unexplained activity occurred then.

Lillian and two lady friends from Bala were sitting in a room on the main floor when something quite mysterious happened. Lillian recalled it this way. "The time was 20 minutes past 2:00 p.m. — I know because I'd just glanced at the clock — when the three of us were startled by a bang on the front door. There was a pause, another bang, a pause, and a third and final bang. Then everything was silent except for people moving around trying to find out what had happened. There was not the slightest trace of wind outside, and Fred couldn't find any sign of young people playing a prank. To this day I wonder whether E.B. returned in some way to give me that signal."

Lillian and Fred Sutton continued to operate the hotel as a place for holidaying families. Despite changing times, they resisted suggestions to sell liquor to their patrons, thereby honouring E.B.'s agreement with Mr. Burgess.

As Hitler and the Nazi party rose to prominence in the 1930s, the name Swastika and the swastikas engraved on the exterior of the hotel became an obvious public relations problem. Hitler's swastika, the reverse of the original design, had become a symbol of Arian supremacy and anti-Semitism. Heritage awards that hung in the lobby were trashed by local citizens and, the Suttons, sensitive to the feelings of Bala residents and customers alike, had the engraved swastikas cemented over and the name of the hotel changed to Sutton Manor in 1939. The war years brought fewer families to Sutton Manor and the Suttons decided to sell in 1943.

E.B.'s grandson, Lillian and Fred's son, Bob Sutton, resided in the former Sutton General Store until 2011 when he passed on. Bob had spent the early part of his childhood growing up and working in his parents' hotel. He was extremely proud of his family. His home told the story of the family: walls adorned with family portraits, old books, and artifacts. His heart was always full of memories. If his kindness and hospitality were any indication, the hotel must have been a warm and friendly place.

Although Bob was a young boy at the time his parents owned the hotel, he still remembered the staff saying "it was magic." What they were referring to, of course, was a feeling that someone was there watching them work in the hotel. He confirmed that there was unexplained activity in the hotel in the 1930s and 1940s.

After his parents sold the hotel, it changed hands a few times and was variously known as Bala Bay, The Cranberry House, and the Bala Bay Inn. The successive owners felt no obligation to honour the original agreement between E.B. Sutton and Thomas Burgess. Once the hotel was sold and liquor was served, hauntings became a regular occurrence.

Tiffany and Ken Bol operated the hotel as the Bala Bay Inn from the 1990s to 2004. In the summer, rooms were available for guests and in winter only the restaurant was open. In all seasons they offered the same hospitality that was there with the Sutton family.

In 1996 I entered the front doors of the 32-room hotel. I could sense the history of the building. The first thing to catch my eye was the elaborate staircase leading from the main lobby to the second floor; a set of doors to the left led to a lounge with a central stone fireplace. Here, the Suttons entertained guests and held festive dances on Saturday nights. At the back of the hotel was the original dining room, where E.B. Sutton lay in state. On the right was the doorway to the bar where once there were rooms for rent. The back section of this bar area had been family quarters for the Suttons.

Tiffany and the staff openly shared their personal experiences with me. They agreed that "stuff" happens, but theories abound concerning numbers and identities of the spirits. Is it Thomas Burgess, E.B. Sutton, old hotel guests, someone simply in love with Bala?

Tiffany was a skeptic in the beginning, "I didn't believe in that at all. A month ago I arrived at work with my 18-month-old son, Shayne. My office is located on the second floor of the building at the top of the stairs. When I reached my office door I suddenly realized that I had left my keys downstairs. I remember trying the door, just in case. Sure enough, it was locked. I left Shayne by the office door and rushed downstairs to get the keys. When I returned, to my amazement, the door was open and Shayne was in the office in the toy box. Who opened the door and took him into the office and set him in the box? I shuddered in disbelief. Was it a ghost?"

Swastika hotel, early 1920s.

Near the entranceway to the Sutton's former quarters people often see something. Tiffany clarified this, "People see shadows in one particular spot in the kitchen. You can actually see the form of a person."

"Activity" in the building can be felt or heard in several different areas, including a number of hotel rooms. In room 319, the room in which E.B. Sutton died, the housekeeping staff always have problems. The television can be heard when no one is occupying the suite. The staff turn the television off, but in a few minutes it's back on again. The room is often disturbed by some unseen hand. Tiffany was working one afternoon in the room when she heard the rattle of a bag in the hallway. "I thought it was another worker so I yelled, 'Hello,' but no one answered." It's not uncommon for the staff to clean the room and return later to find their work undone. The curtain gets pulled halfway across the rod. Sometimes when the door is closed you can hear the curtain moving back and forth.

Who lives in this room? As I walked around the room I tried to sense some presence but was unable to detect anything. The room seemed vacant and like any other.

This was not the case when an unsuspecting family rented room 312. They were the only guests on the third floor. All but the father went out.

He was alone in the room when he decided to have a cigarette on the fire escape right next door. On the fire escape he heard a rumble coming from the room and then the door to room 312 began to rattle. As soon as he put his hand on the doorknob, it stopped. He returned to his cigarette. Again the rumble and the doorknob began to rattle. This time he fled down the fire escape to the ground floor.

During the winter of 1993–94, when air conditioning units were being removed from rooms, a staff member entered room 312. He found the television set on. He tried to turn if off but the switch would not work. He leaned over to unplug it and to his dismay — it was not plugged in!

The second floor has been the scene of unexplained activity as well. Tiffany said, "One day a staff member was showing a room to some prospective lodgers. The hotel employee put the master key in the door lock, turned the key, but there was a force pushing on the door from inside the room. Flustered and understandably embarrassed, she went to the front desk for help. When I reached the room, I had the same experience. The door refused to budge. We found another room to suit the customers' needs." Presumably, an uninhabited room.

Room 208 is notable for sounds of people walking about the room — always when it is officially empty. Staff and visitors have also heard footsteps of people walking up and down the hall on the second floor, perhaps a man and a woman.

In the mid-1980s a group decided to get to the bottom of all these so-called hauntings at the Bala Inn. Their intent was to contact the spirits, identify them, and assist them to leave. One can never anticipate events when exploring the spirit world. One should expect the unexpected. Just so this night.

They gathered around the table in the dining room — the room where E.B. Sutton had been laid in state; candles were lit casting shadows around the room. They waited for a sign. And they got it!

The candles suddenly went out. They sat expectantly there in the darkness. Then the doors in the hotel began to open and shut very loudly. The noise would have been incredible with 32 doors opening and slamming shut. The group fled out the front doors, no more enlightened than before.

Kris Wydra is an amiable man who worked at the hotel on and off from 1992–1996. He handled a number of different jobs and in 1996 he was the cook. Kris definitely had some connection to the spirits in the hotel. Not a day had gone by that he hadn't experienced some form of unexplained activity. He believed that once you had worked in the hotel, it was a struggle to leave. He felt there were many spirits there who had an enormous effect on him, but he added, "I love this building. Every day is an adventure. Sometimes when I'm sitting at a table out in the bar area, I feel a hand on my shoulder. Somehow, I sense that the spirit is attempting to comfort me."

In the mid-90s Kris had been responsible for the security of the building. It was not uncommon for him to spend the night in the hotel alone. Many times, in the late evening, he would hear footsteps up and down the hallways. He never saw a full figure but, what he did see, was the dark outline of a person and a glow around the outline.

He was strongly attached to the building and he felt that the energy in the hotel drew him in. He also felt that the spirits in the hotel wanted to communicate with someone. "I was doing my prep work one morning when four or five times in the span of 20 minutes, someone would open the door and call my name. After the fifth call, I left the kitchen, went into the restaurant area and told the waitress to stop bothering me," Kris said.

She had not called his name at all!

Half an hour later, she arrived at the kitchen door and told him to stop calling her name. There was no explanation. They were the only two people in the hotel at the time. Later that same day the phone rang. Kris picked up the phone and heard someone breathing on line three — just a prank call. Then he realized that line three had never been connected! For the rest of the day every little thing that could go wrong did go wrong.

Each time Kris closed up the kitchen for the day something would happen to him. He felt "they" did not want him to leave at the end of the day. "One summer I lived in the front of the building on the third floor. Every night I closed the hotel and then made a round to check that all the lights were off. Shortly thereafter I would discover rooms still lit. Sometimes a repeat round would bring the same results. I was the only living person in the building," said Kris.

During renovations of the hotel there were several unusual incidents — paint brushes disappeared from one floor to be found on another. Something or somebody would stand over you as you worked.

The central dining room of the hotel, once the lounge and dancefloor, has a lovely stone fireplace. Kris said there were days when it was impossible to light a fire in it. It simply would not start. As far as Kris was concerned this area was off limits, especially after 10:00 p.m. He refused to go there. He explained, "I sense such negative activity in this room after 10:00 p.m. at night." A picture of E.B. Sutton was hanging in that lounge and Kris swore that the eyes of Mr. Sutton followed him. "It's an eerie feeling," he said.

There have been several negative encounters in this same room. One manager was cleaning the salad bar after a busy dinner hour when a broom from the corner of the room suddenly flew through the air, across the room and struck her on the head. Guests at the hotel have seen a woman appear in the area. Several of them have seen this woman walking around the room, as if looking for someone or something. No one knows who she is.

I was taken through the kitchen, the back room, and the pump room beneath the building. Kris was convinced that one spirit inhabited the back room of the kitchen. It was not uncommon for glasses to inexplicably smash on the floor. I sensed that I might have an experience in this area myself. The pump room is at the end of a narrow, dark passageway and I felt somewhat unnerved as we headed there. To add to the effect, the door on the room was the original door to 319 (a haunted room). I was told that stray animals lived here at one time but that one day they just stopped coming. We experienced no activity there, but the tension in the air was palpable.

As we re-entered the kitchen, the hair stood up on the back of my neck and my shoulders felt very cold. Kris turned to me and asked, "Do you feel it?" He had no sooner asked the question when an ashtray at the back of the freezer flew across the room and dropped at our feet. "This goes on all the time," was Kris's only comment. For me, it was a shock, a thrill and a moment of triumph. To write about ghosts is one thing; to experience them is quite another. Now one of the stories of the Bala Bay Inn was my own.

The photograph on the cover of the Bala Flyer shows holidaymakers at the C.P.R. station in 1916.

I was, however, soon to acquire another story. We had a book launch that fall at the hotel. Bob Sutton joined me at the table in the lobby.

We had no sooner started to get settled when the lights began to flicker. "E.B. is here. I knew he'd show up for this!" said Bob.

In spring 2006 Kim Ward and Chris Grossman purchased the Bala Bay Inn with the intent of creating a first-class inn in Muskoka. Their plans involved establishing a new interior look. The entire building was renovated and modernized without losing the historic flavor of the building. In May they opened their doors to the public.

Neither Kim nor Chris is concerned about the ghost stories surrounding their inn. In fact, they are not afraid to promote them. The main lounge on the first floor of the inn is aptly named the Ghost Lounge. The ghostly activities have continued since the first investigation was recorded in *Haunted Ontario*.

Pauline Levesque is head of housekeeping. She has been employed at the inn since 2004. According to Pauline, "I don't believe the hotel is haunted. I have never seen anything."

Although Pauline does not believe there are spirits in the building, she did reveal some stories she had been told by fellow staff members.

About two years ago, staff encountered some unexplained activity in the Ghost Lounge. Pauline described what happened. "There was a table set up in the Ghost Lounge. The table was laden with dishes. The staff working on the first floor heard a crash in the lounge. When they entered to investigate they discovered broken dishes on the floor by the table. No one had been in the lounge at the time.

"Staff would complain they heard voices on the second floor, but nobody was there. I am just waiting for something to happen to me."

Dave Fraser is a jack-of-many-trades who has worked at the Bala Bay Inn from 2004–2007. He was originally hired as a cook. In 2007 he was made head of security and maintenance for the building and grounds. Dave is a firm believer in the spirit activity of the place. He knows from experience.

"When I worked late at night in the kitchen, I would often see a movement out of the corner of my eye. I always felt it to be a female presence — an older woman. I would see her standing by the doorway of the kitchen. It was as if she were keeping watch over the kitchen."

Dave saw a little girl sitting on the steps of the landing in the main lobby.

He explained, "She was wearing period clothing — a large flowing dress. She was about eight-or ten-years-old. She was seated on the third step. Her hair was long. She looked so real. Although we didn't make eye contact, she was there for several seconds and then vanished. I only saw her once, during the first year I worked here."

One time Dave was cleaning the french-fry-maker in the kitchen. There were two nuts on the bottom of the machine. Dave removed them and set them down on the counter. Then he went to the sink to wash the parts of the machine. When he returned to the counter the nuts were gone. He spent several minutes looking for them. Then, to his surprise, he caught sight of them back on the french-fry-maker. Someone had started to screw the nuts back on. Dave was alone at the time, or so he had supposed.

A couple of years ago a guest who was staying on the second floor remarked to the desk clerk that an oddly-dressed woman was walking the hallway. She, according to the guest, was dress in outdated clothing. He went on to describe her attire. A few months later the staff was able to identify the woman's outfit after studying Bob Sutton's photo album. Bob pointed to a picture of three women wearing the same outfits. They were staff uniforms worn during the 1930s.

Glen Hill was the chef for the inn during the 2006 year of operation. Glen, like Dave, believes: "I have always kept an open mind. There is a greater power present. You don't just die, you continue elsewhere."

In June 2006 at 5:30 a.m., Glen was setting up for the Sunday brunch. He was the only one up at that time of the morning.

"I was setting up and heard my name being called. The voice was quite clear. I answered. There was no response. Since I was the only one there I felt in that moment as though someone had walked over my grave.

"About four days later I was in the kitchen in the early morning hours waiting for the rest of the staff to arrive. Suddenly two spatulas fell off the front of the grill. They had been there in a secure position for the morning. That confirmed to me that I wasn't alone."

Staff have recently had an unnerving experience in June 2007. A staff member was attending to all the closing up duties. He made sure that all the candles and lights were extinguished in the Ghost Lounge and the doors locked. A few minutes later he returned to the lobby and noticed a beam of light coming from underneath the door of the Ghost Lounge. He proceeded to unlock the door. Upon entering he was shocked to see one lamp on and one candle burning on a table.

The inn has welcomed the people who take the Wednesday evening summer ghost-walk tour with me (Terry Boyle), and have given us the use of the Ghost Lounge at the end of each tour to tell stories about this hotel.

There is more than one spirit here, for sure. Certainly E.B. Sutton could be one of the spirits in the hotel. He did communicate with Lillian from the other side, as they had agreed. Thomas Burgess was opposed to alcohol and maybe he's watching out for things. The maids may have stayed to help out but it's almost as if a parallel world is happening simultaneously, or is it parallel time?

The Ghost Road

~ Port Perry ~

OVER THE YEARS MANY PEOPLE HAVE TRAVELLED TO SCUGOG ISLAND'S Ghost Road, near the community of Port Perry, to see a mysterious light that haunts the somewhat deserted sideroad. Many claim the spirit of a dead and headless motorcycle rider still appears on this lonely stretch of road near the shores of Lake Scugog.

Sometime during the late sixties, according to local lore, a terrible accident took place here, on this road that runs north-south between the Ninth and Tenth Concessions. Since the road is seldom travelled, many romantically-inclined young people find it a convenient place to park. A long stretch of road such as this tends to appeal to anyone with a yen for speed. As the story goes, a young motorcyclist from out of town chose to test his speed here one night. Travelling southbound and much too fast, he suddenly caught sight of the end of the road, the Ninth Concession. Approximately 100 metres from the south end, near a large, old willow tree, he lost control and barrelled off into a corn field where he struck a rusty wire fence and was decapitated.

Island Road resident Allene Kane, who lives just north of the Ghost Road, believes in the existence of the ghost. Mrs. Kane was quoted in the *Port Perry Star* in 1988: "I don't know why, but there's definitely something out there, a spirit of some kind."

A number of years ago Mrs. Kane had invited two psychics to investigate the "ghost light." Many people had seen (and still do see) a small red light, just a few inches in diameter, supposedly the tail-light of the bike, moving south down the road. Mrs. Kane said, "When we see the light coming toward us, he's returning up the road (near the willow) to turn around, gather speed, and tear down the road and back into the field. I was standing on the road when this red light just simply went right by me about three feet away."

The two psychics agreed that there was a presence on the road and it was a young man in his early 20s, with curly light brown hair, riding a motorcycle and wearing a gold helmet. A third psychic from Oshawa visited the site three times and also sensed a presence on the road. She even felt she knew his name: Don or Dave Sweeney.

Mrs. Kane herself admitted to seeing the light several times and firmly believes it to be the headlight of the motorcycle. Naturally, the Ghost Road is frightening to her. Even during daylight she prefers not to travel the road alone. Her fear escalates when she is near the overhanging tree at the south end of the road, the spot where the motorcyclist lost control. She and her son saw an apparition there, together, one summer morning at 6:30 a.m. She described the experience this way: "A very large, ugly, mangy, humongous black cat appeared out of absolutely nowhere. Now, I'm a great cat lover but I didn't like this cat. It walked down the centre of the road toward the car. I backed up and it kept coming, I backed up again and kept backing up, but the cat still came. Finally it backed me the full mile to the north end of the road, looking at us the whole time." Mrs. Kane felt that the cat had been an embodiment of the negative spirit of the place.

In 1984, Matt Grant, a Port Perry high-school student, parked on Ghost Road with his girlfriend and two other couples. He thought it would be a great idea to scare the girls with the story of the decapitated ghost rider. He got more than he bargained for when he had the most frightening experience of his life.

They were in the only car parked on the Ghost Road. For one hour they sat, waiting for the light to appear. Suddenly the dashboard lights lit up and the radio began to turn on and off. Everyone in the car started screaming, especially when the door locks began to move up and down on their own as well. Matt later said, "The crazy part of this was that I didn't know what to do. You see the keys to the car were in my pocket. I couldn't believe this was happening to us. Next the headrest started rocking me back and forth in my seat and then it ended." To add to their fear, Matt said that wolves were howling during the whole ordeal.

Some skeptics are convinced the ghost light is just a case of car headlights, travelling down the hilly West Quarter Line, which runs almost directly in the same north-south line as the Ghost Road. They think that when a vehicle travels down the West Quarter Line, at an elevation of more than 1,000 feet, it appears on the lower Ghost Road as a single light coming out of the darkness near the treeline, slowly moving downward and seeming closer than it really is.

In July 1983 Cathy Robb, a journalist with the *Port Perry Star*, began an investigation into the Ghost Road story. Ms. Robb contacted a retired Ontario Provincial Police officer, Harold Hockins, who had patrolled the island for many years. Mr. Hockins told Ms. Robb, "I've policed the island since 1954 and I've never heard tell of any fatal accident involving a motorcycle." Ms. Robb also interviewed the psychic who tried to put a name to the ghost; this psychic pegged the time of the accident at 1973 or 1974. The community hospital records for the time, however, revealed nothing.

In August 1983 a ghost hunting team gathered at the newspaper office in Port Perry armed with walkie-talkies, CBs, a camera with infrared film, two cameras with regular film, a high-powered flashlight, and three vehicles. Part of the group with walkie-talkies and CB radios set up on the Ghost Road.

The other members of the group drove up and down the West Quarter Line. Their headlights soon appeared on the Ghost Road as one light floating out of the night sky. Then they stopped, turned off the headlights, and figured they had just put the phantom out of business.

Then the radio started chattering. "Okay, we see your lights," said a voice on the Ghost Road.

"We don't have our lights on," replied the group on the West Quarter Line.

"Well, we see the light."

In 1986 six Niagara College film students showed up to do a short documentary and capture the ghost light on film. The first evening everyone prepared for the arrival of the floating light. One student, stationed in the field at the south end of the road where the rider supposedly hit the fence, claims a sphere of light the size of a basketball popped out of thin air and hovered about 60 feet away for a few seconds.

The students not only managed to photograph the light, but to video tape it as well. When the photograph was developed it revealed the fuzzy outline of a human figure bathed in a strong white light — an aura. On the video take the figure is more defined and appears to have legs.

One of the students, Richard Douglas, stated, "We were shocked, quite frankly. It could just be a one-in-a-million sort of thing, but whatever that shape is, it's certainly coincidental."

Perhaps the next time you find yourself travelling east on Highway 7A, out of Port Perry, sometime shortly after dusk, you will head left up Scugog Island and test your own ability to see the lights on the infamous Ghost Road.

The Jester's Court
Restaurant and Pub

~ PORT PERRY ~

… And he could roast and seethe
And boil and fry
And make a good thick soup
And bake a pie.

Chaucer, "A Cook"

CAN YOU SEE IT, THE GRAND OLD HOTEL THAT SITS ON THE HISTORIC main street of Port Perry? Most people have lost sight of it and see instead the building that has taken its place — a restaurant and pub, once the Murray House, now The Jester's Court. The old hotel is no longer visible yet something remains — the people who once inhabited it!

Imagine for a moment, this hotel as it once was — a two-storey wooden structure with white lace curtains flowing in the window breezes, a genteel lifestyle long-forgotten. Enter by the front door and see the large main foyer graced by an elaborate oak staircase leading to

The Jester's Court Inn as it appears today.

the second floor. To the right is the elegant dining area which overlooks a sparkling stream and the main street. A parlour is located to the left where the amazing price of 25 cents fetches a gallon of whiskey. As evening approaches, the hotel staff routinely lights the candles on the tables and on some of the window sills.

A young couple, here for the night, are seated at the far end of the dining room overlooking the street. They converse with an elderly female staff member with bright eyes and greying hair. A white cotton apron hangs to her ankles. Her job is to welcome guests and to serve them delicious meals. Her smile is genuine and infectious. A single candle flame illuminates the moment.

A young girl plays on the staircase landing with some imaginary friend, all the while taking in the activity around her. She thrives on the bustle of the hotel but somehow she is unnoticed by those around her. Perhaps she is the daughter of the hotelkeeper. The confectionary store in the same building offers a host of merchandise. No doubt the little girl in the hotel craves some of these sweets.

The first building on the site was built by a mason, James Good, who erected a workshop and residence on the property in 1859. He sold the property to Daniel Ireland in 1865 and he turned the building into a hotel.

At the time, Port Perry was a going concern. In 1871 the community received a major boost when the Port Whitby to Port Perry railroad was completed. Additional surveys of lots had been made, property greatly increased in value, and large additions were planned to meet the demands of rapidly-growing businesses. Hotel owners were delighted by the development. What could possibly happen to halt this progress? Fire!

Two fires in less than a year destroyed the Port Perry business section. The first fire broke out in the Thompson House, then known as Ruddy's Hotel, in November 1883. Except for one small hand engine, there was no fire extinguishing equipment. Most of the buildings were wood frame and the fire spread quickly. From Ruddy's Hotel corner along the north side of Queen Street, the fire spread to McCaw's Jewelry store and everything was burned. With winter fast-approaching little was done toward rebuilding, and what the fire of 1883 missed, the fire of 1884 did not.

At 20 minutes to 12:00 p.m. on July 3, 1884, a large fire started in the sheds of Ben McQuay's hotel, which stood on the site of the present-day post office. By daylight, every place of business on the main street was in cinders with the exception of William Tummond's store and this hotel, then owned by Daniel Ireland.

The community rallied to face the devastation of its town. A shortage of nails and building supplies contributed to a slow start. In time, however, life continued as it had prior to these two incredible fires. Meanwhile, Daniel Ireland's hotel maintained its services to the town.

Its time was to come, however, and tragedy struck one winter evening when a fire began in the adjoining confectionery store. The fire brigade quickly responded to the emergency. In the attempt to save the hotel, one firefighter, Joseph DeShane, was struck down and pinned by burning timbers. Although the crew came to the rescue quickly, Joseph sustained severe injuries. One eye and half of his face was severely disfigured for life. In a few hours there were but ashes and charred stone foundation remaining.

Downtown Port Perry after the horrific fire. The building in the background is one of the only ones that remained standing.

Downtown Port Perry, facing east, after rebuilding at the turn of the century. The building located at the end of the row was one of the few to survive the fire.

No newspaper accounts of the fire are to be found — as a result of yet another fire in the newspaper office which destroyed several years of newspaper files forever. No one is left to tell the story of this tragic hotel fire. Had any guest or hotel workers died that night? Will we ever know? For many years the property remained vacant, the old foundation hidden from view by vegetation.

After the fire, Daniel Ireland sold the property to Andy Campbell who built a carpentry shop on the land. In 1913 James Carnegie purchased the property from Campbell, tore down the workshop and built a new, two-storey, red-brick house the following year using the old foundation for the new home. James and Louisa Murray bought the house from Carnegie and the dwelling became known as the Murray House. The Murrays raised a large family there. James was the manager of the Osler Estate south of the causeway. The Murrays left one day, as people do, and in the 1950s a man with the same last name rented the house. He had three children who all slept in one bedroom.

The first reported ghost sightings occurred in the house at this time. Apparently, an elderly female ghost would check in on the children at night. She was a benevolent presence and the children felt very comfortable with her. The youngsters saw her on several occasions and openly referred to her as their night visitor. The Murray family eventually moved out of the house.

In 1979 the Murray house became a tea shop and restaurant and the property once again became a festive centre in Port Perry. Was history repeating itself? Rumours of ghosts began to circulate around town during this period. Had the first Murray family kept the haunting a secret or were they unaware of the spirits in their home?

Carol Morrow and Peter Kirk operated the establishment and subsequently sold it to Whitney and Mark Freeman. The Freemans were unaware of hauntings upon purchase, but not for long!

"We had just bought the house when one night the dog went crazy. Our dog is normally quite passive and well-behaved. This night the dog ran through the kitchen door and down the back hall. We followed her and she eventually arrived at the entranceway to the sun porch. She was baring her teeth and snarling. She went to table 13 and started barking. We didn't know what to think. We had just moved in. We were not aware of the ghost stories," said Whitney.

Mark admitted that he became quite annoyed, "I had the place rewired when we bought it. Then every light in the house reversed itself, but not at one time. We would be sitting in a room with the light off and it would suddenly come on. We had to reverse the procedure of the switches. I called an electrician in, but he had no explanation. You had to believe that something was going on. There was no logical explanation."

The Freemans shared their experiences on *The Dini Petty Show*. Mark spoke of two occurrences that particularly intrigued him. One occurred on the second floor of the house by the attic door. In those days the Freemans operated the business on the first floor. The second floor and attic space were used for living quarters.

"I used to have an office on one side of the attic door and a living room on the other. It only took three steps to pass from the office to the living room, past the attic door. One day I noticed the attic door open. It shouldn't have been open since a deadbolt lock always kept it shut. I locked the door and went into the living room. About three seconds later I turned around and noticed that the door was open again," said Mark.

One year Mark and Whitney decided to take separate vacations. "I intended to leave for my vacation the day after Whitney returned from hers. By now I was quite aware of spirit activity in the house. This particular evening I was going downstairs to the basement. At the bottom of the stairs a light switch was positioned approximately five or six feet away. I told them 'I'm going away for a couple of days and I know that you like to disturb Whitney. I don't want you to do anything while I am away. Is that understood?' The moment I said 'understood' all the lights on the bottom floor came on."

Whitney had experiences as well. "She woke me up out of a deep sleep. I had never seen her, but I had heard and felt her. I knew it was a woman. It was a woman's voice calling out my name."

Whitney's pet rabbit slept in a cage in her bedroom. The cage had a water bottle attachment and made quite a noise when the rabbit took a drink. When that happened at night, Whitney would get out of bed and remove the water bottle. As the bottle started to rattle one night, she rose to remove it. Then Whitney remembered the rabbit was up north with other members of the family. There was no cage and certainly no water bottle. Had the rabbit always been responsible for the noise in the past or did someone else like to "rattle the cage"?

Stairway at the Jester's Court Inn.

The Freemans sold the business in 1986 to Niki Bainbridge who continued to operate the establishment as a restaurant and to reside in the upstairs of the building with her family until 1997. In that period Niki developed an incredible relationship with several spirits inhabiting the house. Niki often saw the apparition of a thin woman in her 70s. She wore a high-collared blue dress and a long, white bibbed apron. Niki described the clothing as late 19th century. This ghost always had a "heavenly" smile and displayed nothing but kindness in her eyes. Her presence was reassuring and somehow comforting. "When I saw the woman I felt her saying that I never needed to worry. Then she would turn around and walk right through the wall," said Niki.

One day a dinner guest in the restaurant saw a little girl sitting on the stairs to the second floor. The girl was playing with a doll. The man thought the girl was real. He had no previous knowledge of haunting in the building and was very surprised to discover that there were no children on the premises.

One night Niki was sound asleep in her bed in the attic; she awoke to hear heavy breathing. She quickly turned on the bedroom light. A glance to the other side of the bed revealed the shape of a human figure outlined in the duvet beside her. Seconds later she watched as the figure disappeared and the duvet returned to its normal flat shape. A ghost had actually joined her in bed!

Another night she was startled from sleep by someone shouting her name in her ear. At first she paid no heed to the noise, rolled over and tried to go back to sleep. Then it dawned on her. Could this be a sign of danger? Rising from bed she quickly scrambled downstairs to check her children on the second floor. They were fine. All this time the thought of fire played on her mind. Her fear took her downstairs where she discovered a candle burning against a wooden window sill. Somehow a mysteriously lit candle had fallen against the pane of glass and then onto the sill. Had the spirit not awakened her the entire family might have been trapped by fire. The original fate of the hotel could have been repeated!

Who lit the candle? The spirits, of course. It was not uncommon for Niki to come downstairs in the morning to find a burning candle on a dining room table. Indeed, Niki once encountered a lit candle every morning for 30 days in a row! Once she even discovered a candle burning under a table. She had had enough. Like Mark Freeman, she decided to address the spirits. Niki asked them to stop; she demanded that they end this ritual and they listened. For a time the candle nonsense was curtailed.

The spirits found other ways to taunt Niki, however. She found herself locked in her room one night, from the outside. She had to call a friend in the morning to come and unlock her bedroom door.

Despite the number of pranks they played on her, Niki felt the spirits in the house cared for her. "After working all day and evening I would stay up to watch television and then nod off. The spirit would turn the television off. I would wake up, turn it back on and shout at them, tell them I was not finished watching the tube. Then I would doze off and waken to find it turned off again. I know they were looking out for my welfare."

One evening after closing time Niki sat down at her desk on the main floor to do some bookkeeping. Suddenly she felt that somebody was watching her. She turned and saw the figure of an old woman standing in the downstairs hall. The woman smiled at her, turned, and disappeared down the hall.

The infamous "Table 13" at Jester's Court Inn *looks* innocent.

When Niki was out for an evening a young male staff member worked late in her place. He phoned Niki to come to his rescue; he couldn't handle the ghostly activity. He saw a couple sitting at table 13 and an elderly woman serving them dinner. The restaurant was officially closed at the time. The lights had been turned off in the dining room but somehow a candle had been lit at table 13. He wasn't long in finding another place to work.

Table 13 is located in the glassed-in porch, overlooking the main street. It was not unusual for a passerby to see a candle burning at table 13 and a couple having dinner — after closing hours. Niki had many requests from diners to be seated at table 13, famous in the area for its "special status."

In late 1997 Niki had to make a heartwrenching decision — continue to stay in business or sell. She was tiring of the long hours and all the hardships that go with owning your own small business. By now she was quite attached not only to her business, but also to the spirits who lived in the building. Nevertheless, she decided to sell. How did the spirits feel about the change?

Apparently they were not happy to have Niki depart the premises. At one point when discussions were being held in the restaurant regarding the sale to the new owners, a plate from an overhead shelf flew off and broke into three pieces in mid-air. One piece hit Sam Chiusolo, one of the prospective buyers, on the head, and the other two pieces landed on the other side of the room.

The new owners decided to change the name of the business and expand it to include a pub. They called this business "The Jester's Court." A lovely interlocking brick patio with a black iron fence was installed in the front. The second floor, formerly living quarters, was renovated and is now a pub, complete with dining tables and a large bar. The washrooms are located on this second floor down a hallway near the stairs.

Scott Chiusolo helped to manage this busy establishment. He was soon introduced to the spirit activity that continued to be a daily occurrence. The large front door to the building has top-bolt and bottom-bolt locks. No keys exist for the bottom lock so the business is locked nightly using only the top-bolt lock. About once a month Scott would arrive at work in the morning only to discover that the key would not open the door, because the bottom bolt had been locked by some unforeseen hand.

"We have often heard footsteps coming down the central staircase. One night I was by myself in the office in the basement when I suddenly heard footsteps coming down the stairs. I got up to see who it could be, but discovered that no one was there," stated Scott.

Joanne Chiusolo was cleaning the ladies' washroom one day when she heard a creaking sound as the door to one of the washroom stalls opened and closed three times. It has also not been uncommon for the washroom stalls to be locked on their own. Many female patrons have had the experience of entering the ladies' room and watching the stall door close on its own followed by hearing the lock being positioned into place. Two female customers saw the elderly woman dressed in blue walk into the ladies' room and disappear right in front of them.

One night Sam locked up and was headed home when he remembered some important papers. As Sam opened the front door on his return, he was grabbed from behind and held in a bear hug for 12 to 15 seconds. He felt quite cold — and needless to say, terrified.

On another occasion he was downstairs in the basement adjusting a compressor when he was pushed from behind.

Other employees of The Jester's Court experience "sightings" or "unexplained activity." Salt and pepper shakers move from table to table, the radio and the lights are turned off and on, dirty dishes are moved from one table to another, pens and eye glasses are taken and a chair is placed on the stairway landing at night. Windows remain open and are unable to be closed. The gas burning stoves and the overhead ventilation fans in the kitchen turn on and off by themselves ... and the list goes on. Certainly a number of pranks involve candles — fire — a strange coincidence considering the history of the building.

Spirits always seem to be attracted to one or two individuals. The reason for this is unknown; perhaps these individuals are more sensitive to the energy. Niki was one and Debbie Burton is another. Debbie has had some incredible and quite hair-raising experiences.

For Debbie it all began back in October 1997 when she was hired as a waitress at The Jester's Court. At the time she was quite aware of all the ghost stories circulating in town about the place, but she paid little heed to them. One of her first experiences was being locked out of the restaurant after finishing her evening shift. She was standing outside on the front porch when she heard the bottom bolt move into the lock position. She threw her hands up in the air and said, "Oh, fine, lock me out I'm finished for the day anyway!"

On another occasion she escorted the last group of people out of the building at closing time and locked the front door. As she turned around to go back into the main room she discovered that some force was holding the door to that room shut tight. Debbie was unable to turn the doorknob. She started shouting, "Let me in. Stop playing this game. I have to close up." The door suddenly released and she was allowed into the room.

When Debbie would arrive to open up in the morning she would unlock the front door and then proceed to go down into the basement to switch on the lights. It was not unusual for Debbie to return upstairs only to discover that some lights had remained off. She may have gone through the ritual of going downstairs to turn the lights on and back upstairs three or four times before all the lights remained on. She often scolded the spirits about the lights. One night at closing time she went downstairs to

Debbie Burton, a waitress at the Jester's Court, has experienced several supernatural encounters.

turn the lights off for the night. When she arrived back upstairs the lights were all on. At that point she confronted the spirits, "If you want the lights on I'll leave them on." She shut the front door and headed home.

One of the most unusual stories Debbie related to me concerned a friend who refused to believe that this building was haunted. It was lunch time at the restaurant when Debbie sat down for dinner in front of the main floor fireplace with some of her friends. The skeptic asked Debbie if she could share her so-called ghost stories.

Debbie related some of her experiences to them. The skeptic said, "I still don't believe that ghosts exist in this place." At the moment the salt shaker flew off the table and landed right in front of him. He was astonished. Then a number of small framed prints on the wall by the table turned sideways. Debbie said, "Look at that!" Then the pictures moved back into an upright position. The friend was now convinced.

If the pictures on these walls could speak ... They do move, however, which was enough for one visiting skeptic to change his mind.

On yet another occasion, Debbie was having a discussion with a female customer by the north facing wall. Two elderly couples were seated nearby enjoying their dinner. The woman asked Debbie, "Do you have ghosts here?" Before Debbie could respond a picture on the wall near the elderly couples suddenly tilted sideways. The couple exclaimed, "They really are here!"

One Sunday night Debbie was serving the last couple in the dining room. They were seated at table 15. All that was left on the table were two wine glasses, a carafe, and two coffee cups. When the couple finished she escorted them to the front door. When she returned to tidy up, all the items were on table 16.

The pub area on the second floor was usually open at night. In May 1998 some security professionals from a nearby casino had decided to drop by for a drink there. They were seated at a table when the elderly woman appeared out of thin air and began to walk toward their table.

Twice this happened. During the second visitation the men fled, shouting at Debbie, "She's after us — the lady."

"I'll talk to her if you like," Debbie replied.

They even left their drinks behind. This same group registered a complaint at the town office with regard to allowing a haunted business to operate in town.

Karen, who worked as a cook in the restaurant, has her fair share of stories to tell concerning the spirits. One night she turned the gas stoves and overhead hoods off and walked a few feet away when she heard the fans turn back on. She shouted to Debbie, "She's turned the hoods back on."

Debbie shouted, "Shut them off." And the hood fans shut off. Karen and Debbie then turned their attention to filling the ketchup bottles and the kitchen fans went on again. They returned to the kitchen and found the fryers on as well. Debbie gave the spirits a lecture. "When you play with fire, you get burned. You could burn the place down. So you had better stop it now."

One night Karen and Debbie were cleaning up the night dishes. Debbie was standing by the bar in the main room. Karen caught sight of something. "I thought I saw a shadow moving by the window. So I stood up and looked over and saw a woman wearing a long navy blue dress. She started to move into the central room and then disappeared right in front of me," Karen said. That same night Debbie heard two people giggling and laughing in the kitchen, but she had had enough for one day and waited outside the building for her ride.

It was not unusual in this place of business to answer the phone and find no one was on the line; or to have heard the knocker on the front door go bang, bang, bang. One of the ghosts even enjoyed whistling and could be heard in the dining room. The music of choice is classical. Just ask anyone who works in the restaurant and they will attest to the fact that the radio sometimes changes to a classical station, apparently on its own.

Returning to The Jester's Court years later I discovered that Deena Vallieres, who was working as the manager back in 1998 is now the owner of the restaurant. I was excited to discover that Debbie Burton, the waitress I had interviewed years ago, was still employed at the restaurant. I spoke with Debbie to see if she would grant me an interview. She agreed and added that she had quite a few new experiences to share.

The restaurant has been physically altered over the years. The small bar area on your left as you enter the building has been enlarged. The kitchen that was adjacent to the bar is now located in a new back wing of the structure. Some tables and chairs have been replaced with booths. Overall, the dining establishment has maintained its cozy and homey atmosphere. The restaurant specialties that continue to draw diners from far and wide are prime rib, slow roasted and served au jus with Yorkshire pudding and liver and onions, baby beef liver, pan-seared and served in red wine gravy with bacon and onions.

I met Debbie Burton on a Thursday evening. Still very animated and willing to share her stories, she immediately launched into a ghostly situation that occurred a few years ago when a film crew arrived in Port Perry to shoot *Welcome to Mooseport,* featuring Gene Hackman. Debbie told me, "It was Friday afternoon around 12:30 p.m. when three film crew members arrived for lunch. One man in the group was a short Scottish gentleman. During lunch the Scottish gent got up from the table and proceeded to go up the stairs to the washroom located on the second floor. A short time later I saw him come down the stairs. Suddenly he stopped. He was having a fit. He began to stammer and shake and I could see beads of perspiration on his bald head.

"I asked him, 'Are you having a heart attack?' He couldn't talk. Then he pointed up and muttered, 'Ghost Lady upstairs.'

"I said to him, 'relax, this spirit likes you.' Then I proceeded to give him a brandy to calm his nerves.

"Then he told me that he was upstairs in the washroom, washing his hands, when he looked in the mirror and an elderly female spirit was looking back at him. She was laughing at him.

"The Scotsman and his companions did manage to eat their lunch; but the group were not filming that afternoon and decided to go to the casino on Scugog Island after lunch."

Guess who went with them?

Debbie added, "I knew our female spirit had gone with them.

"A few hours later the film crew returned. The Scottish man had won three jackpots! He had this huge roll of money. I knew his good luck was a result of our kind female spirit. Then he said to me. 'I just wanted to come back and thank her (the female ghost) for my good luck.'

"So he went back upstairs to the washroom to say his thanks. He also gave me a generous tip," stated Debbie.

More people have reported seeing the spirit of a little girl in the restaurant. Often children who visit the establishment see her standing on the staircase landing that leads to the second floor. Debbie never saw her, not until the year 2000.

That night Debbie and some other staff members were alone in the bar area at closing time. One of the staff had Debbie's digital camera and decided to take a photograph of the group.

At home later that night Debbie and her husband, who is the chef at the Jester's Court, decided to take a closer look at the group picture that had been taken earlier.

Debbie described what happened next, "There we were looking at the photograph. We couldn't believe it. There was the little girl spirit in the corner of the photograph. I was astounded. She was wearing a white Victorian night gown. She had blond hair with bangs. She also had a large piggy turned up nose with deep set eyes and full cheeks."

Debbie explained what happened to the photograph. "We had a friend who owned a good graphic computer and quality printer. We decided to have him make some prints of the picture. Unfortunately, before he could complete the task someone broke into his house and stole his computer equipment along with our ghostly picture. It has been lost forever."

How unfortunate! What are the chances of that happening? Debbie still had more stories to share involving this young girl spirit.

"One time we had two families from England who had daughters, aged eight to ten. Both families had come for dinner. During the dinner the two little girls left the table to go to the washroom upstairs. Who do you suppose they saw? The little girl spirit appeared on the landing in front of the girls. I caught sight of the two girls standing on the landing. They seemed quite animated and appeared to be having a conversation with someone that I could not see. I knew then that the girls were talking to our young female ghost.

"The girls eventually returned to the table and told their parents about seeing and talking to a little girl.

"The parents called me over to the table and said, 'Our daughters tell us they have found a friend.' I told them that they had encountered our little girl spirit."

Every time the two English families arrived for dinner the daughters would return to the landing to talk to the young girl.

For years now Debbie has maintained a close relationship with the elderly female spirit who wears her grey hair up in a bun and appears throughout the building. Debbie explained, "One night I saw her. It was Friday night and no one was seated in the dining room. I was behind the bar with a group of customers, seated and standing, in front of me. Then I caught a glimpse of her. She appeared in the dining room window located in our enclosed porch area. She was looking right at me and motioned with her arms to come and see her. I excused myself from the bar and went out to the porch to see what she wanted. By the time I got there she was gone. She was just playing with me.

"Another night at closing time two chefs and I heard something. Most of the lights were already turned off. We could hear our female ghost walking down the second-storey stairs. We could not see her, but certainly her footsteps were loud and clear. Down the stairs she came and then back up the stairs."

There is another spirit seen at the Jester's Court. It is a man. Debbie has never encountered him, but a couple seated at table 15 did, one Saturday afternoon.

Debbie explained, "The couple at table 15 called me over. They said, 'You know there's a male ghost here.' They continued on to describe him. 'He looks like Rhett Butler in *Gone with the Wind*. He is quite handsome and has a handlebar mustache.' One staff member has also seen him standing by the bookshelf in the dining area. They said he looks like Captain Highliner."

Occasionally spirit activity occurs in the bar area. One of the spirits enjoys throwing glasses behind the bar. Just last month Debbie was the victim of a ghostly physical assault. "I was standing behind the bar, the wine rack was behind me and some other bottles of wine were standing on the counter near the rack. The bar area was full of customers at the time. Suddenly a full wine bottle flew off the shelf and struck me in the back and then crashed to the floor and shattered. The customers at the bar watched the whole thing happen in disbelief."

Debbie continued with tales of ghostly activity, "Two chefs, the dishwasher and I had just closed the restaurant for the night. We had shut all the lights off and the radio. We all decided to go out on the back porch to have a cigarette before locking up. Just as we got outside all the lights came back on and the radio. Someone or something changed the radio station and turned the volume up, then down and back up again. At this point the dishwasher fled down the porch steps, tripped, and tumbled to the ground."

Debbie's relationship with the spirits in the building continues after all these years. She summed it up. "When I go upstairs I talk to them and within a couple of days, spirit phenomena will begin to happen in the restaurant."

Occasionally the spirits are helpful to Debbie. For example, "I was walking upstairs with my arms full of paper towels and bathroom tissues. When I reached the washroom door someone opened the door for me."

What do you think? Are these spirits from the hotel days? Some townspeople and restaurant employees believe the elderly woman is the first Mrs. Murray. What about the couple who dine at table 13 and are waited on by the grey-haired woman? Hotel guests? That is how it seems.

Perhaps we can peak in a window and catch sight of the shadows of yesterday and of others who have gone before and have a word before the curtains are pulled once again.

One thing is certain. We cannot assume that what we see is what everyone else can or does see.

The Inn at the Falls

~ Bracebridge ~

IN MEDIEVAL TIMES THE WORD "INN" MEANT A PLACE OF SHELTER, comfort, peace, and a refuge from outside elements. That meaning is the same today at places like Inn at the Falls in Bracebridge.

There is a woman who gazes out the front second-storey window in room 105 at Inn at the Falls. You might think she is a guest of this fine old Victorian inn that overlooks the tumbling falls and tranquil Muskoka River, but you would be mistaken. To some she seems a figment of their imagination, and to others she is as real as they are. She may appear at any time and any place on the property. Does she walk alone in her own peaceful world? Apparently not!

This inn is a place of tranquility, as a former guest so well expressed: "Words fail me in trying to describe the beautiful time I have had here at Inn at the Falls. It is truly one of the most healing places I've ever experienced … due partly to the sheer beauty and gentleness of the atmosphere, but also — and to an even greater degree — because of the

An early photograph of the Inn at the Falls unearthed by the author. The woman at the window is believed to be there still. The children may be the ones still heard playing in the corridors.

wonderful people who work here.

"They are genuine, warm, open and caring people who make this house a happy and loving home. And there is something profoundly beautiful about their ministry.

"I arrived here feeling exhausted and drained and left feeling deeply refreshed after only three days. I thank you with all my heart for this place of shelter and peace. How I look forward to returning in the spring."

Quite a testimonial! And notice that the visitor mentioned the word "healing."

Located in the heart of Ontario's "cottage country," the Inn at the Falls has a congenial, small-town atmosphere with one of the prettiest views anywhere and it offers a fine selection of accommodation from the traditional to the contemporary.

This is a grand old structure with stone at the front, brick at the back, a large verandah overlooking the Bracebridge Falls and a flagpole on the turret that once flew the Union Jack. It was originally the private residence of John Adair, who sold it to William Cosby Mahaffy in 1877. Mahaffy was only 29 years old and was about to open a law practice in Bracebridge. In 1888 he was appointed the first District judge of Muskoka and Parry Sound.

Ships that steamed the Muskoka Lakes at that time docked just below the home. The original Mahaffy estate extended from present-day Dominion Street along the riverfront to Manitoba Street. Here the Mahaffys raised three sons, Darcy, George, and Montegue. The boys became part of the established business life of Bracebridge, which had just begun to blossom.

Originally called North Falls, Bracebridge was renamed in 1864 when the post office was opened. Some say Bracebridge got its name from Washington Irving's novel *Bracebridge Hall*. Other theories connect it to Bracebridge in Lincolnshire, England. Regardless of its origin, this idyllic location on the Muskoka River, with its unlimited supply of water, was bound to grow.

Bracebridge was incorporated as a village in 1875 and by the 1880s had become a thriving centre for lumbering, manufacturing and the tourist trade, complete with two large tanneries, a grist mill, a woollen mill, a flour mill, and a sawmill. In 1887 the population rose to 1,600 and in 1889 Bracebridge became a town. The Mahaffy family were finely woven into the fabric of this growing community. William died in England on June 14, 1912, at the age of 64. The Mahaffy family remained in the home until the 1920s, when they sold the house and estate.

For a short time the house served as an apartment house and then as a youth centre. Subsequent to that it sat vacant and fell into disrepair. What could be the cause of the decline of such a fine home? Did it, in fact, have other "occupants" who made newcomers and potential owners nervous?

In the 1930s the estate was purchased by a Toronto family who opened a hotel business called The Rainbow Valley Inn. Unfortunately, health problems prevented the owners from having a successful venture. It reopened in 1943 as the Holiday House when Ernie and Marion (nee Timmy) Allchin and Mrs. Wise bought the house and made some additional renovations to accommodate 35 guests. Travellers from all over the world visited the Holiday House in Bracebridge. Notations in the guest book of the stately old mansion included such comments as "My home away from home" and "A wonderful time spent here, hope to return".

To the people of Bracebridge, the Holiday House was much more than a fine hotel and a place for out-of-towners to hang their hats for a couple of days. It had become a cherished landmark.

In the early morning hours of October 20, 1955, fire broke out in the top floor of the hotel. Despite the efforts of local firemen the flames spread through the upper part of the building. Some furniture from the lower rooms was saved but the loss was estimated at approximately $40,000.

Rebuilding started immediately. The stone walls were retained but the rest of the main building was replaced by a more modern structure. Architect Ken Cameron, then in his 70s, designed and supervised the reconstruction of the front portion. The flavour of the old structure was maintained by including features like the Egg and Dart design over the 160-year-old fireplace, the wooden banisters leading upstairs and the three-foot-thick foundation.

Gerard Simmons, a former employee of a business that operated there, was quoted in the local newspaper in 1976, remembering the decaying mansion from his boyhood. "We use to call it a haunted house. Of course, I don't believe it was ever haunted, although Mrs. Allchin, who, with her husband, later bought the house and converted it into a hotel, often said she could hear 'bumps in the night.'"

Mr. Simmons also remembered Mrs. Mahaffy. "It was rumoured that an entire room in the house was devoted to the storage of her hats only. My mother was a milliner at a shop downtown, and she served Mrs. Mahaffy often. She recalled her as a very hard woman to please, who really loved hats."

In 1962 the Wise Room was constructed to create an English pub in the Muskokas. Formerly the furnace room, renovations necessitated the lowering of the floor. The room, supported by thick beams, was created within the original structure. The basement may have been a summer kitchen at one time and later, for the most part, had been abandoned. When the renovations occurred, the old area was again disturbed. This seems to be significant in the development of "activity" in the buildings.

In 1975 Holiday House changed hands yet again, from the Allchins to the Nivens. Jim and Jackie Niven and Jim's grandmother owned and operated the establishment. Jackie passed away in the house after suffering from cancer. Apparently Grandmother Niven was noted to say, "This place has a mind of its own. If the place does not like you, your stay will not be long." In 1983 it was taken over by Arthur and Sylvia Richardson with the following philosophy "To provide old-fashioned hospitality from arrival to departure."

Grandmother Niven's words rang true for the Richardsons. For three long years they experienced constant activity. Cathy Morrow, who worked for the Richardsons said, "Ashtrays would fly off the table and things always went missing. Clothes would fly out of the closet and often disappear, never to be seen again."

Cathy was the office manager and had worked at the inn since 1983. She experienced more spiritual activity than anyone else. She could immediately sense a presence the moment she opened the front door of the house. She revealed that generally there would be a period of increased activity, always early morning and late night, followed by a period of no activity — and then the cycle would be repeated.

Early one morning during her first year at the inn, Cathy was downstairs in the pub. To get to the pub one had to walk down a set of stairs, past the main desk, turn left, and walk down a long, limestone corridor to the pub entrance. There was a small room for guests situated at the end of the bar. The pub washrooms were located in the lounge by way of a small corridor at one end of the room.

Cathy said, "I had just reached the corridor when a woman suddenly appeared in the doorway. She was so vivid. I could describe everything she was wearing. She had on blue jeans and a red and white striped T-shirt. She was a small woman with shoulder-length dark brown hair. She would have been in her 40s. I just looked at her and within seconds she vanished into thin air."

Cathy told her story to the housekeeper when she arrived for work. "You have just described Jackie Niven," said the housekeeper. It seemed that Jackie, who had died in the house, had never left. There was no other explanation and there may never be one.

In Cathy's experience, the hauntings occurred primarily in the early morning or late at night. Her day would start at 5:30 a.m. She came through the front entrance and passed the formal dining room on her right and the parlour, complete with a fireplace, on her left. She continued down the hallway past the main central staircase until she reached the front desk located at the end of a short corridor.

The beautiful Inn at the Falls in the summer.

One morning Cathy arrived during a loud thunderstorm. There was an eerie feeling of foreboding as she approached the front door. She sensed a presence as she entered the inn. This sensing would start as a feeling and then become a knowing that something was about to happen. The "feeling" came this time, from the dining room. As she entered the darkened room a sweet, faint voice said "hello". There was nothing to be seen but later that day another staff member said it had been the spirit named Sarah.

There have been several sightings of a young woman with long, dark brown hair in the inn. "Sarah" is sometimes only visible from the shoulders up and usually appears in white. She is seen in the main hallway and in the lower level stone corridor leading to the pub.

In 1988 the inn, now 17 rooms, was purchased by Peter and Jan Rickard. A new name, Inn at the Falls, reflected the unique location overlooking the falls. Their long experience in the hotel industry, combined with their keen desire for a family business made the inn the perfect venture for Jan and Peter. In 1989 they began to expand the inn to include other houses on their cozy village street, including the former Salvation Army Citadel.

Each year their business grew to make it one of the most successful in Bracebridge. The inn featured 37 rooms and suites, some with whirlpools and fireplaces and most with balconies that afforded views of the surrounding gardens and Bracebridge Bay.

The Rickards openly admitted that the inn was haunted. They even printed a light-hearted warning on their menu: "Our three resident ghosts, Bob, Charlie and Sarah, are friendly spirits and tend to keep mostly to themselves. Bob inhabits the kitchen area, Charlie the upstairs corridors, and Sarah can be heard rustling through 'Victoria's' (dining room) on occasion."

In 1995 Geraldine Page, a well-known American psychic (not the famous actress with the same name), arrived at the inn for lunch. On entering the premises she was immediately drawn upstairs. There she sensed the presence of a spirit and, before lunch was served, made arrangements to come back and "make contact"!

She arrived on Saturday and was ready at 10:00 a.m. in room 105, where the woman can be seen in the window. Peter Rickard recalls the early moments, "Just as she began, the lights dimmed on their own. Geraldine was lying on the bed and slowly drifted into a trance-like state. After a very short time she awakened, overwhelmed by the number of spirits that approached her. She said the spirits were there to be healed!" How many spirits did she see? What did she mean that they were there to be healed?

Ms. Page saw the woman sitting in a chair at the window of room 105. She appeared to be looking out at the street and the grounds. There was another woman moving back and forth in the hallway. She seemed concerned for the unborn child she was carrying. A man walked beside her attempting to comfort her. Ms. Page was also surprised at the number of children in the house. The voices of children laughing and giggling in the main hallway of the inn had been a common occurrence, although there had been no recorded sightings of them.

So many spirits in one place hampered her efforts to connect and the session ended. Is the atmosphere there a healing one? Do the spirits sense a presence that might help them? Is there an opening there to their world? One thing is certain: there have been many spirits seen in various areas of the inn.

The strangest experiences, however, occur in room 105. This was the former bedroom of Judge Mahaffy. Most guests have experiences out of the ordinary in this room. Some guests feel a presence the moment they enter

The Inn at the Falls in the winter.

it. Room 105 is a spacious suite. An antique bed is situated on the left as you enter; the bathroom is to the far right and a central fireplace is located on the west wall; the east wall has a bay window with two chairs and a table, and a chandelier hangs over it all. It is in this room where a woman can be seen sitting or standing by the window that overlooks the street. The spiritual activity in this room varies — the television turns on and off by itself and missing keys from other rooms often show up in room 105.

In early September 1993, a couple who had honeymooned at the inn returned for a weekend getaway. They arrived Friday evening. That day the housekeeper had placed her master key in the door while she proceeded with her chores. This was the usual procedure. However, this day the key disappeared while she worked. A hunt produced nothing. The couple were informed about the missing key and they too had a look for it — to no avail. On Saturday night when they went to retire, the key was found beneath the covers in the middle of their bed.

A guest from room 106 expressed her concern at checkout time: "How is the pregnant woman feeling who is staying on the second floor?" She had overheard a conversation in the hall between a man and a woman. The guest in question had the only room booked on the second floor that night. This had happened to several guests and staff.

Monty Mahaffy, centre, in 1903 with some friends who included Frank Bastedo, second right, later Lieutenant-Governor of Saskatchewan.

Two women arrived for lunch one day and introduced themselves to Peter Rickard as the Kirk sisters who had lived in the house for a short time in the 1930s. They had heard the stories about the hauntings at the inn and had come to set the record straight. As far as they were concerned the place was not haunted.

Peter was amazed at their skepticism. Nevertheless, he told the women the story about the pregnant woman who can be heard walking the second floor hallway at night. The sisters looked aghast and turned pale. Their father's first wife had fallen down the stairs when she was at the end of her pregnancy and she and the baby both died in the fall. It was their turn to be shocked.

It would also appear that Judge Mahaffy has remained connected to the hotel. Although he died in England in 1912 he seems to like it at the inn in Bracebridge. Cathy Morrow first saw him in November 1997.

Cathy had seen the portrait of the Judge that once hung in the main hall. Early one morning in November Cathy was serving breakfast downstairs in the pub. As usual, Cathy had opened up that morning. The pub room was open and she had returned there after completing her other morning chores. As she walked down the corridor, she caught sight of Judge Mahaffy by the cubby hole. He was floating about six inches off the floor. Cathy said "He appeared as he had in real-life, wearing grey pinstriped pants, back shoes and a large black tailcoat. His face was the same as in the portrait. Then he vanished."

This wasn't the first time the Judge had been seen in the pub area. At Christmas, 1996, John, the general manager, was closing up for the evening when suddenly a well-dressed man walked past the bar and into the back room to the washroom area. John waited patiently for the "guest" to finish in the washroom. Finally he went to find him. There was no one to be found and no other way out! His description fit that of Judge Mahaffy.

In spring 1998, Samantha, the duty manager, was in the little room to the left of the pub entrance and about to turn off the lights when she heard a voice say "Don't turn the lights out!" She was the only one there.

The kitchen is another area of unexplained activity. It would seem a spirit (who the owners have jokingly named Bob) inhabits this area. Although Bob has never been seen, he does like to let you know he's there by throwing pots and pans across the kitchen. There are no theories about the who, what, or why of Bob.

A rather difficult guest complained, when he was leaving, of a kick to the backside on the stairs. He wanted an explanation. It seems quite ironic that what he received from a spirit might seem to be just what his behaviour warranted.

Kevin Poole, a well-respected book wholesaler in Ontario, listened one summer evening in the early 90s to the staff at the pub talking about a spirit in residence at the inn. The bartender said a woman, incredibly true-to-life, was often seen in the corridors. Kevin scoffed slightly at the bartender. He wouldn't discount spirit activity, but to actually witness what looks like a human being was unbelievable to him. Kevin left the pub, he assured me, in a sober state. As he approached his car he saw a beautiful, young woman with flowing brown hair in a long white gown. She walked past Kevin as he turned to open the car door. It was the woman from the window of room 105, the woman the bartender had been talking about! Kevin walked to the rear of the car, in order to follow her, but she had vanished into thin air. Kevin still remembers his sighting very clearly and emphasizes the woman's youth, beauty and the fact that she was so vivid and disappeared so completely. He was in awe of what had happened and felt that she had appeared to him in order to prove her existence.

The ownership of the Inn at the Falls has changed since I was last there in 1998. Stonecroft Management now (2007) owns this inn along with several other resorts in the Muskoka District.

The General Manager/Innkeeper is Krista Havenaar. Krista has managed the property for the past three years. I was curious to hear her perspective concerning the existence of spirits at the inn. "I don't know. I really don't know. It is so hard to believe." This skepticism persists despite several personal experiences with the ghostly activity in the inn. Her first encounter occurred in 2004.

"I was setting up for a wedding in the front parlour during the fall of 2004. I began cleaning and then moved some furniture around. I turned the heat off in the room. The thermostat was located just behind the door. After adjusting the thermostat I placed a sofa against the door, concealing the thermostat. I turned on some music. I left the room to go to the kitchen to get some glasses for the set-up. When I came back to the parlour it was stifling hot. I put my hand on the heat radiator and it was pumping out heat at full blast. I also noticed that the music had been turned off.

"So I turned the music back on. Then I pulled the sofa back from the door to check the thermostat. It was on full. I turned the thermostat off. I moved the sofa back against the door and went to the kitchen. This happened three times in a short period of time and I finally spoke out saying 'that is enough' and it stopped."

Krista is well aware of the mischievous antics of the spirits in room 105. She recalled one incident. "A few months ago we had a woman staying in room 105. She phoned the front desk stating that there was no remote in the room for the television. Our staff delivered her a remote. In the morning there were two remotes on the night stand."

Krista Havenaar, General Manager at the Inn at the Falls, Bracebridge.

On another occasion Krista encountered a female spirit in the kitchen. "One evening I was walking from the front desk to the kitchen. The time was 11:30 p.m. Just as I was entering the kitchen I heard this young woman's voice just a couple of feet behind me say 'hi.' The voice was quite clear. Yet, there was no one in the kitchen. I locked up and left."

According to Krista, "At one time we had this head housekeeper who had misplaced her keys to the other buildings on site. Another housekeeper found her keys in room 105."

Katherine Cumberland has worked as a pub server in the Fox and Hound Pub, located on the lower level of the inn, for more than four years. She has actually seen the ghost of Judge Mahaffy sitting in the front parlour of the main building. Katherine is very happy working here. She is not afraid of the ghostly events of the inn or shy about sharing her stories about the inn. In fact, she knows she is never alone in the building!

Katherine Cumberland, a server at the Fox and the Hound pub, located in the lower level of the Inn at the Falls, Bracebridge.

"I believe that there is something here. You definitely get the sense that something or someone is around. You often get the feeling that you don't belong in a certain area of the pub."

The pub is not the only area where Katherine senses a feeling of unwelcome. "Just down the hallway, prior to the pub entranceway, is the laundry room. You just get a sense of not being wanted there. It's not a bad feeling, but the hair on the back of my neck will stand up."

Another area of activity on the same floor level is the meeting room. Katherine explained, "About two years ago we were going to have a party of guests use this room. Prior to the meeting, a staff member was on their way to organize the room. Just as they approached the room they heard the sound of a table being dragged across the floor. The employee thought the guests had already arrived. When she entered the room it was empty of people. She quickly observed that one table had been mysteriously moved from one end of the room to the other end."

Guests who stay overnight upstairs in the inn still encounter unexplained events. Katherine related how one gentleman spent a restless night here.

"About two years ago we had a man staying upstairs in the main inn. At 11:00 p.m. that night, the last staff member locked the front door and left the premises. During the night the guest was awakened by people running up and down the hallways. He thought it was children playing. When the staff arrived in the morning this male guest, upon leaving, bitterly complained about not having been able to sleep for the noise. He soon discovered that he had been the only guest staying in the inn that night. The front doors had been locked and had not been possible for anyone to have entered the building."

Some evenings when people stay at the inn, they have reported seeing Judge Mahaffy just standing in the building. He is usually described as wearing a jacket and vest. There are other reports of a child you don't see, but hear.

Katherine has encountered this child. "One morning I arrived at the pub and heard someone say 'hi' to me. The voice belonged to a child. I looked all around, but couldn't find anyone. This happened twice in one morning."

Some staff members believe the child sounds like an eight- or 12-year-old.

In the past few years guests taking pictures of the front parlour report capturing orbs of light floating in mid-air. Even the silhouette of a person has appeared in their pictures.

Breeze Mitchell began working at the inn in the early part of October 2006. She is convinced of the existence of the spirits. Her childhood experiences have confirmed this belief. Breeze recalled that childhood. "You have to know what is real. Death is just another plane of existence. When I was younger we lived in a house in which the previous owner had died. I would see these grey images there. As a child I would sleep walk. My mother would watch me talking to someone that she could not see. I have no memory of this."

Her day at work begins by saying hello to the staff and spirits, including Judge Mahaffy. She still sees these grey images most of the time. Breeze shared some of her experiences at the inn.

"There are three sets of lights in the kitchen. This one morning as I entered the kitchen the sets of lights went off, one by one. In the back of the kitchen the freezer doors will open and slam shut on their own. In January 2007 I was near the back of the kitchen. I looked out the window and caught sight of a woman. She was wearing a large-brimmed hat and wore an old-fashioned dress. She was standing on the outside verandah. Then she disappeared.

"Certain mornings you can often smell the scent of lavender and roses in different areas in the main dining room just off from the central hall.

"One day I had a file disappear in the office. The file reappeared a couple of days later."

Guests who photograph the interior of the inn frequently capture images of orbs. Some people believe these orbs are actually spirits or the energy of spirits. Sometimes they appear with a pattern inside the orb.

Breeze shared a couple of stories surrounding room 105. "In late October 2006 a lady was booked into room 105. She wanted to see a ghost. That night she couldn't fall asleep. Then she felt someone patting her back and rubbing it. She drifted off to sleep. When she awoke she realized that she was alone and had as she had wished, encountered a spirit.

"In November 2007 we had a male guest staying in room 105. A couple days later he came up to me at breakfast. He said someone got out of his bed in the middle of the night. He asked me if that was possible? I replied, 'yes.' He took some pictures of the room and photographed an orb floating over the bed."

Most guests who stay on the second floor report an experience of the same paranormal event. Breeze explained, "This one night we had three young boys in room 107 and a couple with a baby in room 105. The other rooms on the floor were occupied by couples. They all reported in the morning that they had heard two gentlemen roaming the halls and going up and down the stairs and slamming the emergency exit door by room 107. The guests could hear them talking about business. This had happened about 2:30 a.m. Every room confirmed this account."

The interview with Breeze ended with this final statement. "Each part of life is a plane of existence. How you handle one plane is how you transfer to the next plane."

It would seem that the spirits at Inn at the Falls are still there. And no wonder, since the inn is truly a place of beauty, peace, and quiet, a place set aside from the hustle and bustle of the world. Perhaps it is too good to leave.

Either the activity here has increased, it is more able to be perceived, or it just needed a more empathetic response in order to manifest a little stronger. Whatever the cause, it certainly proves that people in the third dimension are not the only ones who appreciate a good and peaceful inn.

The Donnelly Homestead

~ Lucan ~

AFTER ALL THESE YEARS THE TRAGEDY THAT BEFELL THE DONNELLY family on the night of February 3, 1880, can still be felt. A group of vigilantes burst into their homestead on the Roman Line, near the village of Lucan, and killed the family in cold blood. Was it a case of murder? Why does this story continue to haunt the imagination of so many people? How many lost souls wander the Roman Line?

These questions preoccupied me as my car made the turn onto the Roman Line. Donnelly investigation, here we come. Once on the Roman Line I saw St. Patrick's Church and my thoughts focused on the surroundings — a community made up of both Irish Catholics and Irish Protestants. Their hatred for one another had not been left back in Ireland. The bickering, the fighting and the bad feelings were very much alive. Lucan, Ontario, like Belfast, Ireland in the 1990s, was a very dangerous place to live in the mid-1800s. I wandered through the graveyard, past old moss-covered monuments with variations of the

Celtic cross and found the Donnelly gravestone. The inscription verified that five of the Donnelly family had perished on the same day. A short distance down the Roman Line was the Donnelly Homestead. What had really happened here?

James and Johannah Donnelly arrived in Canada from Ireland with their first child, James Jr., in 1842. James found work in London, Ontario and a second son, William, was born there in 1844. The following year they settled in Biddulph Township near Lucan and built a shanty on lot 18 of the sixth concession. A third son was born in 1847 and Johannah gave birth to four more sons over the next nine years.

On June 25, 1857, a man by the name of Maloney was having a logging bee. It was at this bee that James Donnelly senior got into a fight with Pat Farrell. When the fight ended Pat was dead. A feud started over this incident. James hid out for some time from the law, but eventually served seven years in the Kingston Penitentiary. He was released from prison in 1865. In 1870 the Donnelly family found four large fieldstones and placed them near the shanty to form a foundation for a standard six metres by eight metres (18 feet by 26 feet) squared-log cabin. In 1871 a large frame kitchen was added to the back of the cabin.

The Donnellys were feared by many in the region. By 1875 the Donnelly brothers were behaving like bullies in the streets and in the taverns in both Lucan and in the surrounding district. The Donnellys had many friends, but had at least as many enemies. Ray Fazakas, in his book entitled *The Donnelly Album* stated, "In all justice it must be stated, said one man who was friendly toward them, they would scarcely stop at anything to resent a real or fancied injury ... so disorderly and lawless a state has the place become that it is often impossible to get magistrates to issue, or for constables to execute processes when required."

It was not uncommon for a Donnelly to use force to get what he wanted. And it was more apt to be a threat to kill than a warning! No constable in his right mind attempted to arrest or rebuke an individual who showed neither fear of death nor any remorse.

In January 1879 Father John Connolly arrived in the area at the request of Bishop Walsh. The Bishop wanted the good Father to investigate all the crimes that had been occurring in the parish. Father Connolly walked the roads of the parish and interviewed people about

William Donnelly built this house on the site of the original house a year after the killings. Robert and his nephew James, son of Michael, are in front. Circa 1901.

barn burnings, animal mutilations, beatings, and thefts that were ongoing in the parish. A grim picture was painted of the violent Donnelly boys.

Father Connolly created a Property Protective Association. Members of this group would go from farm to farm to search for stolen property. This was meant to help determine who was committing the crimes. The association later changed its name to the Biddulph Peace Society. Members met at the Cedar Swamp School on what is now Highway 23.

James Donnelly wanted to join this organization, but his son William persuaded him not to do it. He believed that someone would hide stolen goods on their property in order to see them charged with theft. William was not far off the mark. Already this Society had formed an inner committee for the purpose of determining ways to deal with the Donnellys. The time for action was nearing. When Patrick Ryder's barn was burned to the ground, this vigilante group advised him to charge the Donnelly boys with the crime. Unfortunately for the Society, all the Donnelly sons were accounted for on the night the barn was burned. Ryder didn't stop there; he charged James and Johannah with the crime. Who really burned the Ryder barn down? Was this justice or was it vendetta?

Everyone ended up in court, but there was no evidence to prove James or Johannah had burned the barn down. Justice Grant of the court allowed for one more court date to be set. Ryder and his friends of the inner committee knew full well that the Donnellys could bring false-arrest charges against the men who had been responsible for their trial. This would mean payment of monetary damages to the Donnellys.

The committee met at the Cedar Swamp School to discuss what they should do. They decided to pay the Donnellys a visit on the night of February 3, the day before the next court date. They would tie them to trees and beat them, if necessary to extract confessions for all their crimes. As a precautionary measure they asked James and William Feeheley, friends of the Donnelly family, to find out where the Donnellys would be on that night. The Feeheley brothers were promised $500, the amount outstanding on the elder Mr. Feeheley's mortgage. If the brothers didn't agree, their father would lose his farm.

Meanwhile, the Donnellys had gone to Lucan that day for supplies and to pick up young Johnny O'Connor to house-sit the farm the next day while they were at court.

James Feeheley paid a call at the Donnelly home that night. He talked with Tom, Johannah, and Johannah's niece, Bridget, who was visiting from Tipperary, Ireland. He heard James Sr. talking to someone in the bedroom and thought it was his son, John Donnelly. He also saw that Tom was going to sleep in the bedroom near the kitchen and Johannah was to sleep in her bedroom with Bridget. Feeheley left then and stayed nearby to watch. At about midnight 35 men, led by 28-year-old constable James Carroll, left the Swamp School and headed for the Donnelly home. They met Feeheley and heard what he had to say. The vigilantes surrounded the house.

Constable Carroll gave the men orders to wait outside until he gave them the word to enter. Carroll then opened the door and entered Tom's bedroom. He lit a candle and snapped a set of handcuffs on Tom. Carroll informed him that he was under arrest.

Johannah came out of her bedroom to see what the commotion was all about. She returned and asked Bridget to get up and feed the kitchen fire to warm the place. Carroll proceeded to James Donnelly's bedroom. He told Donnelly that he had another charge against him and ordered him to get up. James got dressed and Johnny O'Connor handed him his coat, one that he had been using as a pillow, but Johnny remained in the bed. Carroll seemed oblivious to Johnny. It was apparent that Constable Carroll was drunk.

Carroll asked James where his son John was. James replied that he wasn't at home and turned to Carroll and demanded that he read the charge. At that moment Carroll shouted and the men surrounding the house charged in, swinging clubs. James was struck first and sank to the floor near the stove. Bridget ran from the kitchen through the darkened living room and up the stairs to the loft. Johnny O'Connor hid beneath his bed. Tom Donnelly ran through the front door where the men who had remained outside repeatedly stabbed him in the back with a pitchfork and clubbed him over the head. Then they dragged him back into the house and laid him down over the hatchway to the root cellar. Johannah was beaten in the kitchen. Even their small dog was clubbed and beheaded. A group of men went in search of Bridget who had hidden in the loft. They returned a few minutes later with her dead body.

Tom groaned and his scalp was laid open with a shovel.

For the finale, they splashed coal oil over the beds and on the floor, set the place on fire and fled up the Roman Line in search of William Donnelly who lived at Whalen's Corners, a distance of nearly three miles. Johnny O'Connor waited no longer and fled through the back door. He remembered hearing Johannah groan but didn't stop to help her. The house burned to the ground.

Robert Salts, author of *You Are Never Alone*, described what happened next. "Many of the men had done and seen enough and set off for home. The inner core of the group pushed on to Will's house.

"Their plan was to go out into Will's rented barn and beat up his stallion. When the horse made noises, the men figured that Will Donnelly would come out and they would club him to death. They beat and whipped the horse but no one came out."

The vigilante group then surrounded Will's house and Jim Ryder called out, "Fire, fire, open the door."

Robert added, "In the house were four people. Martin Hogan, a friend of Will's had stopped by. Martin was planning on threshing grain in the barn of Morkin, a neighbor, down the road the next day. As it was late Will told him to stay overnight, because he would wake everybody up in the Morkin household. John Donnelly was staying overnight to take the cutter and Will and his parents to that final court case in Granton. John and Martin shared the bed in the small room off Will's bedroom.

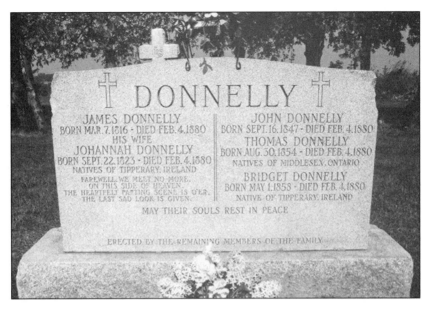

Donnelly tombstone with birth and death dates, including those slain on February 4, 1880. Bridget Donnelly was just twenty-two years old.

"Norah Donnelly was expecting their second child in June and had retired early. When Will came to bed, he asked Norah to move over. She told Will he had to climb over her as she had her side of the bed warmed up. This probably helped save his life, for when the vigilantes pounded on the door, it was John who sprang out of bed. He went through Will's room saying that someone was shouting that there was a fire. John lit a candle as someone called, 'Is that you Will?'

"John responded, 'Yes' and opened the door."

A nervous vigilante saw a figure at the door and opened fire; the shotgun blast blew more than thirty holes in John's chest. Then a muzzle-loading rifle ball went through his lower abdomen. He was mortally wounded and died a short time later. The vigilantes, having shed enough blood for one night, left for their homes. It wasn't until 4:00 p.m. the next day that the coroner arrived at James Donnelly's home. After the ravages of the fire, only two small steps at the front of the cabin remained. It was then discovered that souvenir hunters had already helped themselves to artifacts and body parts. Bridget's head was gone and so was the right arm. Johannah's head had also disappeared. It was reported that when Robert Donnelly arrived the next day from St. Thomas, he kissed the burnt exposed liver of Tom and the blackened heart of his father.

A number of years ago a public school principal was researching the Donnelly story. He received a call from a man who claimed to have Bridget's arm bone and offered to sell it for five hundred dollars!

James Carroll and five other men were charged with murder. They got off scot-free. This is hard to believe today. Even with eye witnesses such as Johnny O'Connor and Will Donnelly, they managed to beat the charge. Did they suffer shame or grief over their deeds? Did they ever come to terms with their crimes or did they take their shame to their graves?

In 1881 Patrick, Will, and Robert Donnelly built another house on the Donnelly property next to where the log cabin had once stood. In fact, part of this new home stood on the former site of the original shanty built by their father. William planted five chestnut trees for the five family members that perished around the site of the log cabin. Two chestnut trees are still there today. In 1939 the property was sold to non-family members.

In 1988 Linda and Robert Salts and their son Charles decided to leave London, Ontario, and move to the country. On Mother's Day they travelled to the countryside and looked at a homestead in Biddulph Township. The house, drive shed, and barn were situated on 6.19 acres that had originally been part of a 100-acred parcel. As they toured the place they noticed six large fieldstone rocks laid out to form a square, just to the north side of the homestead. They later learned that this was the site of the massacre.

Linda knew that they would live there. The district was not new to her. She had grown up two concession roads to the west. They bought the Donnelly homestead and moved there in August 1988.

A few months later Linda began to suffer from depression. It happened every time she worked in the kitchen. The Salts phoned Father Smith of the Catholic Church. They wanted the father to perform an exorcism. They could both feel an unwanted spirit in the kitchen area. A Donnelly perhaps?

The priest was not keen on doing an exorcism, but he agreed to bless the house and provide the last rites for whatever was in this area. It is significant that the Salts' religious background was Protestant, but that they felt strongly that the entity or entities in the house were followers of Catholicism.

While Father Smith performed the last rites, Robert was overwhelmed with a sense of sadness and grief. Over the next several weeks Linda experienced a relief from emotional heaviness.

Robert and Linda have experienced numerous incidences of unexplained activity in their home. Robert awakens often in the middle of the night to hear faint footsteps on the stairs. During their first year Linda and Robert were sometimes startled in the night by a crashing sound. Their first thought was ice sliding off the main roof onto their bedroom roof but when it happened during the summer months they knew that ice was not the problem. They found it unusual that there were no reverberations that accompanied the sound.

In April 1994 Robert's father passed away. Robert was given some china that had been in his family. He and Linda washed and sorted the cups and saucers to place them in a cabinet. Robert explained what happened, "We were interrupted by a telephone call and when we returned to the task of the dishes, we discovered one particular saucer had been placed in the cabinet and the glass door left open."

In the middle of August 1995, Robert not only heard footsteps, but heard his name called three times. "The voice was a soft but firm masculine tone. The time was 1:29 a.m. on the clock radio; I did not respond nor get up to investigate as I knew there would be no one there." One Sunday around noon, Robert was having a shower. He glimpsed the shadow of a person on the shower curtain — it came into the bathroom through the open door and then went back out. Robert immediately turned off the water, grabbed a towel and walked to the living room. Once there he asked Linda and his son Charlie if either of them had just come into the bathroom. The answer was no. Robert and his son tried to re-create the shadow on the curtain but to no avail. No matter how they adjusted the bathroom light, they were unable to make the same moving shadow.

The same day, when Linda was just outside the laundry room window and Robert was on the other side of the house, Linda heard a muffled sentence that ended with several clear words. She said it sounded like, "Is anybody home?" or "Don't you know this is my home?"

At times Robert has been home alone in the living room and heard something. "I hear someone walk onto the deck, open the door at the far end of the house and step in. When I go to investigate, I find no one there! Linda

Contemporary sign outside Robert and Linda Salt's house, the Donnelly homestead.

told me one day that it has happened to her on more than one occasion."

Their German shepherd refuses to go upstairs to the second floor or down to the basement. A small thing, maybe, but dogs and cats are very sensitive to spirits.

One day Linda discovered that the laundry basket had been moved from under the clothesline to a spot across the laneway — a distance of about six metres (20 feet). The basket was upright and a dozen or so clothespins were still at the bottom of the basket. There was two inches of snow at the time and yet there were no footprints.

The Salts have a tremendous sense of history. They have opened their home and property to the public and even provide tours if they are booked in advance.

The barn as it looks today. Built in 1877, the cement foundation was added by Robert Donnelly in 1906.

Robert is a very good tour guide. He loves his subject matter — the Donnellys. When he toured me around the homestead I listened intently to him. He walked me over the murder site and described what happened that fateful night and he showed me where the bodies were found. His storytelling brought the Donnelly family back to life and for a moment I was there and so were they.

Not surprisingly, visitors encounter spirits on the property. Robert described what happens, "Many times when a group is waiting for their tour, I am told that they have an odd feeling that someone is watching from the barn. The barn was built in 1877. This feeling of being observed can occur anytime and anywhere on the property. It can suddenly come over you and you find yourself looking around, expecting to see a pair of eyes staring in your direction."

At one time Linda and Robert allowed people to sleep in the barn — people who were hoping to have a ghostly experience. "One man and his wife told me the next day that around 1:30 a.m. they heard footsteps coming toward them in the straw and he felt pressure on his chest."

In the spring of 1996, two grade 13 students complained of that same feeling of great pressure on their chests. One of the girls said she heard screaming in her head for a few moments while in the barn.

Sometimes people ask, "Who is the man who stuck his head out of the barn door to see who is in the laneway?" Robert's usual response is, "The man is a ghost of someone who lived here. The tourist then usually asks if I'm kidding and I explain that I'm not."

One time they heard the sound of a handsaw. Robert explained, "Linda was taking bags of groceries out of the car next to the driveshed and as she walked by the doors she distinctly heard the sound of a handsaw coming from within. At first, she thought I was home working in the shop, in the drive shed. She soon realized that the doors were locked and I was not at home!"

According to Robert, "There have been times when film crews have arrived with expensive and elaborate video cameras and within a few minutes of taping, the battery pack has lost its power and the videographer is at a loss to explain the drain in voltage. This has occurred several times on the Donnelly homestead and is not just a coincidence. The technician often exclaims that he just put in a freshly-charged battery. It has been necessary to run an extension cord out from the house to keep the camera rolling."

Robert described what happened once to a family that decided to tour the barn on the property. "While at the barn at the end of a tour, a father and mother and myself stepped out onto the gangway and I told them to check the reaction as I slammed the barn door shut while their 15-year-old daughter and her best friend were on the inside taking pictures. In an instant the door flew open and out rushed the two girls. The daughter was stunned to find her father on the outside for she believed he had pushed her out ahead of him. Her eyes grew wider as we all assured her that her father had not been behind her. The girl became very agitated and frightened and wanted to know who had pushed her out the door. There were four distinct marks on her arm as if someone had gripped her firmly above the elbow. I had no idea my attempt at startling the teens would have such dramatic results. The young girl was truly scared and cried and clung to her mother all the way back to the car."

The Catholic Church on the Roman Line where the Donnellys are buried.

Roberts continued, "On a number of occasions when tourists have entered the barn, someone will ask while looking up, 'who hanged himself here on one of those beams?'"

During one tour a participant saw something. Robert described what happened, "While seated at the site of the massacre, a gentleman distracted me during the presentation by staring at some object behind me over near our garden by the barn.

"'Who is that man over there through the trees?' he questioned.

"We looked in the direction he was pointing but saw no one.

"Where did you see him and what does he looked like," Robert asked. Everyone wanted to know who this stranger was.

"The tourist in the group was adamant he had seen a man's face in the bushes next to the garden," stated Robert.

"'I distinctly saw a man looking at me through the foilage over there,' blurted the tourist. 'There was just the face, I didn't see a body.'"

According to Robert, "We all looked again at where he was pointing but to no avail. The face was gone. An eerie feeling came over all of us as we silently looked at one another for a moment. I continued with the storytelling but the feeling lingered for a short while."

When a tour is over it is not unusual for people to tell Robert that something touched them when no one was standing near them. One tourist, a man named Bill Burns, actually sent Terry Boyle a letter a few years describing just that.

"My wife and I have long enjoyed your 'Discover Ontario' radio program and yesterday we bought your first book, *Haunted Ontario*. To be perfectly frank, I'm a bit of a skeptic when it comes to the paranormal but the index entry of six pages on the Donnellys caught my attention. I have had a 30-year fascination with the Donnelly story during which time I had many talks with Ray Fazakas, the author of *The Donnelly Album*, and corresponded for a while with Nora Lord who was William Donnelly's daughter and who died in Sudbury on September 22, 1975, at age 88.

"In June 1997 we paid a visit to Rob and Linda Salts' place on the Roman Line. We did the tour of the property, something I had wanted to do for years but the previous owner was hostile to the idea of visits from strangers and kept the property posted.

"Rob, who claims to be a psychic, certainly has no doubts about the presence of spirits in his home and barn. And something happened while we were there to shake my skepticism, at least somewhat.

"You relate that people touring the site often mention that something touched them on the shoulder while no one was standing near them. I had a similar experience. While Rob was leading us from the house to the murder scene, I felt something brush across the top of my head. My first thought was that a flying insect, a very large flying insect, had gotten into my hair. I patted the top of my head very gingerly so as to dislodge it without getting stung, but there was nothing there. Then the same thing happened again. This time I ran the fingers of both hands through my hair but came up with nothing. I didn't mention this to anyone at the time but a week or two later I wrote to Rob telling him about it."

In fall 2001 Robert described an unusual event that happened in the house. "Our son Charlie, then a teenager in high school, was preparing to go up to bed. He bade his mother and I goodnight and opened the door to ascend the stairs. With the door partly ajar, the sound of music could be faintly heard in the air. I quickly asked Charlie if his computer or stereo was on but he shook his head. The melody stopped suddenly. The music was not modern but was typical of a much earlier time. The sounds seemed to come from everywhere and nowhere in particular. Charlie and I looked at each other in astonishment. His mother in the next room should have been able to hear the music but denied hearing anything."

In May 2007 I returned to the Donnelly homestead to meet Robert and Linda again. It was great to see them and exchange greetings. I was curious to find out if the public were still drawn to the Donnelly story and to this property. Robert shared this, "There is not a day that goes by without people driving by and stopping in front of the house. People are so curious. I have a chain across the driveway when we're closed and people still climb over the chain and knock on our door."

According to Robert, "People come from all over the world. We have even had visitors from as far away as Japan."

The Salts still require their privacy and ask everyone to phone ahead to book a tour. According to Linda their busiest time is during the months of July and August.

Robert and I strolled the property as I took some new pictures. We ended up at the barn. Robert reminded me about the number of visitors that had sensed or physically experienced the spirit activity in this area. He added, "We had this young man who walked into the barn and then became quite ill. He fled the structure and was sick to his stomach outside." Obviously his system was unable to handle the energy that is ever-present here.

The Donnelly story continues to haunt many of us. Perhaps it is because we really don't understand that time in history. Was it really so violent, so lawless? It seems that it was. The Donnellys were representative of the unruliness of the times and the community may have needed scapegoats, outlets for their anger. The Donnellys became a target.

Perhaps the Donnellys were not finished with life or perhaps they still need revenge or is it justice they require? They certainly haven't left the Roman Line. The places themselves, both the town of Lucan and the Roman Line, are haunted by the entire history of the place. Nothing lets the story die and so it lives, on and on — there's more than one way to haunt a place, it seems.

The Canadian Museum of Nature

~ Ottawa ~

THE TRADITIONAL SACRED KNOWLEDGE OF NATIVE PEOPLES HONOURS the existence of unseen powers. These powers are often personified or accentuated by the Great Mystery. Native peoples, in fact, see life itself as power, a mysterious mix of non-material energy, energy which manifests in different densities for each manifestation. Energy then can be found in objects such as thunderstones, charred wood, volcanic stone, feathers, rattles, masks, bones, and medicine bundles. Each plant has a special power and personality, and medicine people learn to communicate with these things for healing and ceremony.

A Teton Sioux man once stated, "It is hard to explain what we believe about this. It is the general belief of the Native peoples that after a man dies his spirit is somewhere on the earth or in the sky. We do not know exactly where, but we believe that his spirit lives ... so it is with Wakan'tanka. We believe that he is everywhere." This mysterious power known to the Native peoples has manifested on occasion in the Canadian Museum of

Nature. Spirits have returned to protect and guard their scared objects — their medicine! It is a story about honour and respect.

This story began in 1905 in the City of Ottawa. In a field just south of the downtown district a massive new building was constructed to mark Canada's coming of age as a modern, scientific nation. They called the building The Victoria Memorial Museum, now home to the Canadian Museum of Nature.

The Museum was founded on the work of Montreal-born geologist William Logan, the first Director of the Geological Survey of Canada in 1842. During his lengthy career he was responsible for sending parties across Canada, collecting plants, rocks, minerals, and Native artifacts. No one at the time expressed much understanding or concern for the sacredness of these objects and the life force they carried. Few believed in these powers and they did not understand how to honour them. It was all done for the field of scientific enquiry.

Logan's growing collection was originally housed in Montreal and after his death in 1881 the 2,000 boxes and barrels of specimens were crated and sent to Ottawa. For several years they were housed in a squalid old hotel in the By Ward Market. The Victoria Memorial Museum Building gave the collection a new home, or so it was believed.

David Ewart, the Dominion's Chief Architect and designer of the building, was drawn to European architectural history and created a structure that was characterized as "free Gothic," "Tudor Gothic" or "Scottish baronial." Ewart commenced to create a fantasy of towers, crenellations, arched windows, trefoils, and false buttresses using local sandstone. The building was completed by 1910 at a cost of $950,000.

Geologists scrambled to fill the empty halls and exhibits were prepared. By 1912 the museum was stocked with minerals, bird and fossil specimens, and Native artifacts.

One tourist at the time described the museum as "an impressive pile of masonry." The building weighed 30,000 tonnes (65,000 tons). Soon this weight presented a problem, as the structure had been erected on unstable clay. The ground began to sink beneath the building, the ceilings and walls cracked, floors heaved, and the great tower began to tilt. In 1915 the problem was solved by removing the upper three storeys of the tower.

In 1927 the name changed to The National Museum of Canada. Over the years the museum was divided into Natural History, Human History, and Science and Technology. By 1968 many of these branches became separate institutions housed in their own buildings. In 1988 the Victoria Memorial Museum Building became the exclusive home of the National Museum of Natural Sciences — now the Canadian Museum of Nature.

The museum building also shared quarters for a time with the government of Canada. After the burning of the Parliament buildings on the night of February 3, 1916, the House of Commons and the Senate assembled in this building until November 1, 1919.

When Sir Wilfrid Laurier died in 1919 his body lay in state in the Museum's Auditorium for three days. His was the only body ever to be laid out here — did his spirit stay behind?

No one is sure how long the museum has been haunted. Perhaps it began when the artifacts were first disturbed or after they were put on display in the museum. Certainly a mysterious energy did and does exist in various parts of the building. This mysterious force is seen and witnessed by the individuals working in the building. It follows people down halls, shadows them, and oppresses them. Sometimes it takes shape and can be seen.

For the sake of privacy and at her request for anonymity, we will call our source "Mary."

Mary has worked at the museum since 1981. In her early years there she heard other employees talk about the hauntings. They would speak of lights going on and off, of doors opening and closing on their own, and of fire alarms sounding on the fourth floor. It was all just nonsense to her.

The museum, at that time, was divided into two different themes. The west side of the building was used for an exhibit of Native artifacts with historical displays on floors one, two, and three, and a folklore exhibit located on the fourth floor. The east side of the building was for science exhibits. Mary told me that most of the unexplained activity was experienced on the west side of the building at that time. At night the cleaners working in the building would find that their vacuum cleaners had been mysteriously unplugged. The elevators in the building would travel from floor to floor on their own. A person entering the elevator would press the button for the floor they wanted and find that the elevator simply ignored this command

and continued on its own up to another floor. Employees would experience varying degrees of temperature in certain areas of the building; they would find the atmosphere to be either too hot or too cold. Yet the climatic controls showed the temperature to be at a normal setting. Others would smell an odd odour, like rubber burning, in the west end of the third floor.

Mary's own experience of alarms sounding, of disembodied conversations and eerie energy started in 1983. There were no logical explanations to be had.

She described the first floor exhibits as ones pertaining to the beginnings of life. They explained and illustrated the work of archeologists, the "dig." Methods of artifact recovery were presented as well as many different relics.

The second floor displayed the history and life of the Inuit and many other Native nations. She recalled displays including a teepee, ceremonial masks behind glass, hunting tools, medicine bags, rattles, bearclaw necklaces, pipes, and sticks with bird heads on the ends of them. Mary always felt uncomfortable when she walked past these exhibits. Something didn't feel right! Could it be this non-material energy — the power of life that is in each object — is that what she felt? Spirits were here, still connected to their medicines — medicines locked up and on display. Totem poles and beaded clothing once worn by Native peoples were located on the third floor. A folklore display was located at the far west end of the fourth floor, which was a split-level floor. Some of the articles were described by Mary, "We had an old Ouija board, books, candles, ladders, suitcases, and an open umbrella on display. One section of the display looked like an attic." She never liked spending time alone in this exhibit. It made her feel very uneasy.

Mary had an extraordinary experience in 1984. "It was five minutes to ten in the morning. I was on the fourth floor in the folklore exhibition area. The museum opens at ten o'clock. After having heard alarms go off in the building and seeing other strange events, I was getting a little paranoid. I said to myself, 'It's okay; the museum is not really haunted.'

"Suddenly I felt someone following me, someone trying to scare me! This feeling grew and grew and I decided to stop in front of a mirror. I thought I might be able to catch a glimpse of the 'spirit.' There was no one else in this part of the building at the time. There I was standing about four feet away from the mirror when a human figure appeared between me and the mirror. I could see the outline of the head, shoulders, and arms that seemed to be part of the same body. The shape was that of a large, tall man. He was enshrouded in greyish fog and was therefore quite fuzzy. My body went cold. Then the spirit approached me. I was rendered completely immobile; not to mention the terror that passed through me when the figure moved right through me. As soon as the 'spirit' entered my body I felt extremely hot. I just watched this form walk through the right side of my body. I remember moving my head around and watching it move a couple of feet beyond me before it disappeared. I just stood there in shock! I didn't know where to go. I eventually ran down the ramp and out of the room. I found a security guard and asked if he had seen anyone leave the floor. He hadn't."

Who was this spirit? Maybe the spirit was in some way connected to an object on display in the folklore exhibit. The Ouija board was the first thing to come to my mind. Had someone used this board improperly? Were they unable to create closure? Do people know how to use these things appropriately?

Mary is not the only employee who has seen a ghostly form appear in the building. She recalled another worker who has since passed away. "She would talk to me about a spirit who appeared on the third floor in the west wing, by the Native exhibits. She used to say he was a young Native person. He was quite clear when he appeared. She said he had large cheekbones and long hair. She could look right into his eyes. He was very friendly and appeared most nights, according to her. She thought he was trying to communicate with her."

In 1989, the museum acknowledged the fact that unexplained activity was occurring in the building. They called in a medium to exorcise the spirits. According to Mary, "The medium went up to the fourth floor of the museum and said a spirit was indeed in the area. She then went down to the third floor to begin her work. In a trance-like state she soon communicated with the Native spirit who always appeared in the Native exhibit area. The medium said his name was Swift Eagle, a Native person who once lived out West. He had died a slow death in the forest after eating some poisonous plants. According to the medium he had arrived at the museum in order to accompany his clothing!"

For some reason Swift Eagle remained there with his clothing. Was it sacred to him? Mary described his outfit on display, "It was a long coat with fringes and pants. A hat was also part of this exhibit. It had feathers and lots of coloured beads on it. The medium then said a prayer and asked him to leave. She began to cry after this. That's all I was told."

Did the hauntings end after the exorcism? No. Swift Eagle was never seen again as far as we know, but what about the spirit Mary had seen in the folklore exhibit? Could there be more spirits roaming the exhibits?

Mary continued, "After the medium had left, we still heard stories of unexplained activity in the museum. I still have days when I feel awkward about entering some parts of the building. Since 1990, the security people have seen a shadow on the second floor and are often touched on the shoulder by an invisible hand.

"We have had some unexplained activity in the Mineral Gallery. It was during the construction of an exhibit that contained a radioactive machine; that we had some experiences. At that time the machine was blocked off from public use. I would be standing in front of the machine when the exhibit alarm would just go off. No one was there using the machine. We also had problems with the exit doors on this floor. The doors would shake or seem to move as if someone was pushing on them, when no one was there."

We were nearing the end of our interview, but I sensed that Mary had something else to tell me. Call it a hunch or a gut feeling, but I knew there was another story about this museum. And so I asked her — and I was right!

Mary took me to the first floor on the east side of the building to show me something. As we entered the Dinosaur Hall I was immediately drawn to the exhibits. There in front of me were several dinosaurs looming over my head. Live plants are used to highlight the various settings in this gallery. Mary walked over to an open space at the far right-hand side of the hall. She looked at me and said, "I have seen a dark, black shadow on the floor in this area. I watched it travel across the floor in a wave-like motion. It was so eerie!"

I shivered just thinking about seeing this "shadow" travelling across the floor in front of me. This was certainly a different experience to have. But Mary wasn't finished! "One time when the contractors were working in this area, a tall plant suddenly bent right over and then flipped back into an upright position on its own." The interview was over but I'm sure strange occurrences in this museum are not.

I clearly saw, here, the existence of unseen powers. Swift Eagle had remained as a result of some connection to the sacred. Perhaps his headdress designated his status or his gifts and some energy around them needed to travel with him to the other side. We know very little about "personal medicine" and how and what goes with a soul to the other side.

As for the museum, we do know forms of spirit activity continue. What is really happening in the Mineral Gallery? Who pushes on the exit doors; who touches the security personnel on the second floor; what creates the shadow that moves across the room in the Dinosaur Hall?

The spirit activity continues, as I learned during a visit in 2007. Security guards now report seeing a dark cloaked figure on the fourth floor of the building.

The Canadian Museum of Nature is indeed a place of unseen power surrounding sacred natural objects and life forms that have been removed from their burial places and put on display. The very essence of evolution binds the living world to the spiritual world. What better place than a museum, to observe and experience both worlds.

Carleton Gaol

~ Ottawa (now the Ottawa Jail Hostel) ~

OUT OF THE SHOWER AND INTO THE CHANGE ROOM ... THE CLOTHES have vanished. In the hallway a sock appears, a shirt ... pants ... belt ... underwear, scattered down the hall like stepping stones. Where is the watch!? The search begins in another room, or more accurately put, another cell. No longer ticking, the watch lies upside down on a cold, concrete floor. The searcher flees to his room. What on earth just took place? These are common occurrences for those who stay in the Ottawa Jail Hostel, once the Carleton County Gaol. Time stops on death row.

In this building, literally hundreds of lost souls wander the corridors, up and down the stairwells, occupying cells, remaining on death row, waiting, waiting, waiting. A noose was always hanging from the gallows, swinging like a pendulum, marking time. Each time it stopped, another unmarked grave was dug in the dusty courtyard. Reports written by the Inspector of Jails in the 1870s bear witness to the atrocities.

This eerie stairwell leads to the quarantine area where immigrants awaited their fate. Many souls welcomed death.

Children cried out. Women wept. Men prayed for their souls as the jailor turned the key. Darkness would blanket the lost and forsaken and smother their torment. A woman dragged into a secret passageway was assaulted. Her cries were muffled. She prayed for it to end. In total darkness naked people were sentenced to six months "in the hole," spread-eagled and chained to a cold cell floor to die without seeing daylight again. What prompted such cruelty?

In 1862 the Carleton County Gaol opened as a maximum security holding facility. Many people were actually innocent victims: men, women, and children. Once incarcerated they were seldom allowed to shower, never given more than one meal a day, never saw daylight, and died in filthy, unlit quarters in the basement, known as the quarantine area. When they died their bodies were burned in the courtyard. Other victims were illegally hung inside the building, far from the view of any governing officials.

Prisoners had no space to move. Their cells had no plumbing or electricity.

Many people died here as a result of societal prejudice against the mentally ill and the poor, and methods of treatment that resulted from this prejudice. To declare a person insane was one such method. The fate of many unfortunate victims rested in the hands of jailors and inspectors of jails. In August 1876 Inspector Christie observed the following, "I found 58 prisoners in custody, 31 males and 27 females. Of the women, 25 were under sentence, one waiting trial and one, Mary McLoughlin, was insane. She appeared to be a fit subject for asylum treatment."

A common example of punishment is recorded in Inspector J.W. Langmuir's report dated September 24, 1877, "Reference has again to be made to the case of Margaret Dogherty, who, owing to outrageous conduct, has constantly to be kept under punishment, being at this time tied to the cell door. Although, properly speaking, the woman may not be insane, there can be no doubt she is a fit subject for an asylum. Sarah Jane Thomas has not yet been certified to be a lunatic and at the time of my visit appeared to be quite sane, although was evidently of weak intelligence."

The Carleton County Gaol closed in 1972 because of lack of sanitation, poor lighting, and unsavoury conditions. In 1973 the building became the Ottawa International Hostel and it is now known as the Ottawa Jail Hostel. Portions of the interior were renovated to accommodate overnight guests but much of the jail remains as it was, including the cell blocks, the gallows, the hole, the stairwells, the secret tunnels, and death row.

Wade Kirkpatrick was the friendly Operations Manager of the hostel. Although Wade had never seen a ghost, he had experienced unexplained activity. "My wife, Crystal, and I lived here for four months before we bought our first house. We lived in an apartment on the seventh floor. We often heard voices and banging on the pipes, although no one was to be seen. People often claim to hear cell doors closing behind them as they walk down death row, which is on the floor above the apartment. One time we went away for a week and shut the water off to our apartment. When we returned from our holidays the water was turned on and hot water was now coming out of the cold water tap."

Guided tours of the building are offered. Carol Devine, one of the tour guides, discusses its history, its mystery, and the hauntings of the jail. I joined Carol on her tour. Come along.

Unmarked graves are said to occupy the courtyard area. It was here jail guards burned the bodies of quarantined Irish immigrants.

The tour began in the basement. Carol usually does not take a group here because it is nerve-wracking. A set of stairs leads down to a room that has the appearance of a black hole. The lights were not working. It was chilling and oppressive. This area had been used as a quarantine station for newly arrived immigrants in the mid-1860s who were thought to be suffering from scarlet fever. In most cases the whole family would be sentenced to the basement of the Carleton County Gaol for no less than three months.

Carol said, "This is where thousands of people died. Whole families would be shoved into this space and left to fend for themselves. Most of the jail guards were afraid to enter the area for fear of catching the disease. I assume their honey buckets (pails that served as toilets) were never removed or cleaned, but rather were dumped in the corner of the room. When residents died, the guards would remove their bodies and burn them in the back courtyard. No one ever received a proper burial."

On we went to debtors' prison. People who could not afford to pay their bills were impounded here. They were sentenced to work in the kitchen and other areas of the jail. Many came with their families who were housed in dormitory-style cells. This section of the building was converted to a chapel shortly after 1920, when the Canadian government abolished such prisons.

Down the hallway there is an entranceway to a tunnel which leads to the courthouse next door. Part of the tunnel has been filled. Carol remarked, "People hear moaning coming from the tunnel. I am certain prisoners were taken down into the tunnel and abused. No one would ever hear their screams." A door seals the sight but not the sounds!

Next, Station 2, solitary confinement, nicknamed "the hole." Six cells were used to house troublesome inmates and they have remained intact to this day. Here inmates were placed for anywhere from one day to six months. All privileges, including visitors, exercise, and chapel, were taken away. Prisoners were forced to use honey buckets instead of toilets. The cells had two doors. The second door was made of solid wood, and no light came through. Prisoners were often stripped of their clothing and shackled, spread-eagled, on the floor. Once a day the guard would unchain them for 15 minutes to eat their only meal and to use the honey bucket. Many inmates died in that darkness. The unlit cells and shackles are still as they were. The suffering in those cells is palpable. Scratch marks are visible on the walls and floors.

At one end of solitary confinement is "A" and "D," now also referred to as Station 3, where the admittance and departure of inmates took place. Here prisoners were stripped of their clothes and personal belongings, taken to the shower, given prison clothing, tobacco, a comb, and a toothbrush without a handle. This is now a kitchen!

Station 4 was originally the visiting area. There are metal screens on the staircase that act as anti-suicide bars. They run up the entire staircase. Although not often actually seen, a spirit haunts this area. The "presence" follows visitors up the stairs and imposes pressure from behind. In 1910 two inmates overpowered a guard and threw him to his death in this stairwell. A menacing presence has remained. I experienced it myself, very strongly.

Station 5 was originally cell block one and two and is now a residence for female visitors. The cells have been enlarged to create dormitories. Sleep well!

Station 6 was the former residence of the governor of the jail, known as the governor's mansion. This is the eeriest place of all. Carol's story gets darker now. A strange spirit, referred to as "the vampire" haunts the back stairwell of this section. For years, prisoners referred to this spirit as a creature who "tries to push your soul out of your body." Carol said, "My grandfather had heard about this vampire. They say it feeds on the sick. No one knows for sure whether this creature's territory extends throughout the jail or not."

Carol recounted the experience of two young men who stayed in the governor's mansion in 1994. "One night one of the men retired early for the night. He awoke suddenly to see a shadow standing in the doorway. He turned the light on, but the bulb shattered. The shadow quickly skirted across the room and disappeared in the corner where a set of lockers stood. Workers later discovered a secret passage right where the shadow had vanished."

Does the "vampire" travel the building through the many secret passageways?

An ominous inscription was discovered on the stairwell during renovations of the building in 1972. It reads, "I am a non-veridical Vampire who will vanquish you all. One by one I will ornate your odorous flesh with famished fangs. But Who? Are there 94 or 95 steps to the ninth floor? A book on the top shelf will lead you on the right path."

This quote is accompanied by a circle with inverted letters. Carol explained that it was decided to preserve the inscription but added, "No one is sure what all this means. We do know that a bookshelf did exist at one time on the ninth floor in the matrons' quarters. The inscription has been here for many years.

"At one time a warden moved into the governor's mansion with his family. His eight-year-old son often played in the stairwell. By the time the warden left the prison with his family, the son was eleven. The child's personality had drastically changed and he was terrified of the dark."

The stairwell is a very strange place to explore. There is a sensation of being watched and there is a heaviness in the atmosphere. Reading the inscription makes the hair on your neck stand up.

No one could be prepared for the visitation of a spirit in the sixth floor stairwell. Here in the stairwell is an arched alcove with a ledge where security guards could chain a prisoner who was giving them difficulty. It is a space now bricked up except for a hole between two bricks.

Something remains hidden behind this wall. A frigid draft can be felt escaping from the dislodged bricks.

In 1994 the authorities invited a group of psychics to investigate the hauntings. They claimed that 13 active spirits existed in the building and another 150 souls returned there on the anniversary of their deaths. This is a phenomenal amount of activity for one building and particularly for a hostel.

Carol added, "One psychic felt very drawn to this wall (the sixth floor alcove). She felt the spirit of a dead prisoner was still here." She suggested that I try putting my hand in the hole between the bricks, something she herself had done. I did it. Not for long, though. It was a moment I'll never forget. My hand felt like ice!

"After the psychics left, things went crazy. Doors would lock and we could hear voices throughout the building. In the evening, after the front offices were closed, the computers would turn on by themselves and begin to print out incoherent pages of text. The phones kept ringing, but no one was there. This went on for three days," stated Carol.

On the ninth floor we entered what was once the hospital and later became the female inmate cell area. It is now the home of two lounges for the hostel. The carpeted area in the lounge was once the doctor's office and the wooden floor area was once the operating room — a disturbing thought.

Carol added, "The hospital area was only used from 1862 to 1867. In those days, prisoners, if they were lucky, were allowed to shower once a month. Infection was a major health problem in the jail. Inmates would often lose a limb as a result of unsanitary conditions. They were given a shot of whiskey to numb the pain while a doctor removed one of their limbs with a saw!" According to Carol, no records were kept and the hospital was too expensive to maintain and it was subsequently closed.

Officials then renovated the area for female and children prisoners. Young boys were jailed here until age 12, when they were placed in a regular cell block in the jail. The women and children were allowed one bath per week and were required to share the bathwater.

Children's voices are often heard on this floor, especially in the lounge where a crib is located today. Wade Kirkpatrick said, "We would often hear noises in the lounge. When we went to investigate all we found were guests watching television with the volume low. Obviously, they hadn't heard anything. Periodically we could hear women screaming here."

In February 1899 a male prisoner escaped to the women's cell area on the ninth floor. From there he fled to the bathroom in the hallway. There were no bars on the bathroom windows at the time. He fell to his death. A second man made the same attempt. Both legs were broken in the fall and he crawled across the street to the City Registry Office. Carol added, "The guards rushed out and across the street and shot him dead." A third prisoner successfully escaped through the same window but was apprehended and shot to death on a street in Ottawa.

Station 8, the original, male cellblock, was once called "the drum." The cells measure one metre by three metres, (three feet by nine feet). There are 20 cells located here. Prisoners were locked inside these cells for 12 hours at night. They spent the other 12 hours of the day locked outside their cells. The hotel has no plans to renovate this area into dorms. This allows visitors to see and feel what a cell block was like. A few people have attempted to sleep in a cell, but have reported an uncomfortable sleep and a deep feeling of uneasiness. This is quite understandable since the gallows are nearby and death row is just on the other side of the cellblock. Clanging cell bars and voices are heard in this area.

Station 9 is death row. Unexplained phenomena and bizarre accidents have occurred in this part of the jail. Death row consisted of four cells, numbered one to four.

Patrick Whelan spent ten months in cell four awaiting his execution. He was convicted in 1869, on circumstantial evidence, of killing Thomas D'Arcy McGee, one of the Fathers of Confederation. Whelan and 18 others were arrested for the crime. The other 18 were acquitted for lack of evidence, but Whelan was hanged for the murder.

During his ten months on death row, Patrick and his personal guard, John Lyle, became close friends. Mr. Lyle believed Whelan was innocent but could do nothing to stop the hanging. Whelan and Lyle still stalk the halls of death row. They have been heard and seen.

There were three official hangings in the gallows here at the Carleton County Goal. Canada's last public hanging was of Patrick Whelan in 1869. There were 5,000 curious onlookers.

There are many superstitious traditions surrounding hangings. People were usually hanged on the 13th day of the month. If that was not possible, then the hanging would take place on the 13th hour of the day. The hangman always stood on the left side of the prisoner because the right was said to be the divine side. The hangman always tied the noose 13 times. Oddly enough, Patrick Whelan was hanged at 11:00 a.m., February 11, 1869.

People staying in the hostel have reported seeing Patrick Whelan sitting in his cell writing at a desk. He may still be writing the letter he wrote to Sir John A. MacDonald to profess his innocence.

Some people believe Patrick Whelan haunts death row because he was hung on the 11th hour, on the 11th day. Other reasons may be his innocence of the crime and the broken promise to send his body to his wife in Montreal.

His gravesite in the courtyard was discovered 58 years ago when the City of Ottawa built the Mackenzie King Bridge and expropriated part of the courtyard that had, at one time, extended a considerable distance from the building. Whelan was identified by a ring on his finger. Construction workers discovered 140 gravesites in total. It is a concern for some that more bodies were buried beside the building and in the present-day parking area.

Former inmates hanged at the jail still remain, haunting death row. One evil spirit is reported to inhabit the corner of the hallways. Lights often flicker and cell doors slam shut in this area.

Death row is reported to be haunted by several spirits. Carol said, "death row is haunted by an evil spirit. No one knows who or what it is. The spirit lives in the corner of the hall. You can feel its presence. The air becomes heavy the way it does before a thunderstorm. The lights flicker or dim. Some visitors see flickering lights along the wall across from the cells. Years ago there were oil lamps on that wall.

"A female visitor attempted several times to open one of the cell doors. The door was sealed. No matter how hard she tried, the door would not open. The cell door had no lock on it. Nothing should have prevented that door from opening.

"The third cell door on death row has been jammed for years. No one can open it. This is the cell where people report hearing three knocks. The psychics agreed that four of the 13 spirits haunting the jail are here on death row. At one time two iron doors were located on either side of death row. They were removed after an unexplained accident. An employee lost a finger when, without reason or warning, one of the doors slammed shut on his finger. One window on death row also shuts all by itself."

A set of showers are located at the end of this hall for the guests who are staying in the hostel. It is common for people who come out of the shower to find their clothes strewn down the hall in front of the death row cells. Personal possessions have been found in the cells, often watches have stopped ticking.

The cell doors clang shut as people pass them. Late one night after conducting a tour, Carol had to return to death row. "This area is so haunted. I was walking down death row, passing the cells, when I came to the cell Patrick Whelan had been in. Even though it was August this one area was many degrees colder. I just kept on walking and didn't look back. In the past we have had a contest for anyone willing to sleep all night on death row. Most people have fled before 1:00 a.m."

Returning in 2007 to the Ottawa Jail Hostel, I learned that the hostel had been voted as "the most haunted building in Ottawa." Only the year before, the *National Post* rated the facility as "the most unusual place to sleep in Canada."

Greg Brockmann is now the Director of Operations. Greg is quite enthusiastic about marketing the history and hauntings of the building. He wants people to know how unusual and special a place this hostel is to travellers worldwide.

A female co-worker of Greg's, who wished to remain anonymous, offered a couple of recent stories surrounding the spirit activity on the premises. Apparently last summer a male employee working the night shift was walking along death row when he heard footsteps behind him. He put the creaking noise down to the wooden flooring but, when he reached the section of concrete flooring, the footsteps could still be heard behind him.

"Six years ago I began to work here. My first experience was during a quiet time in the winter when I and a fellow employee were involved in a fire drill. We were responsible for floors seven, eight, and nine. Our job was to travel the floors and to make sure that no one had remained in the hallways or rooms. We did know we were all alone when walking floor eight, which is death row. By the little door in the hallway we heard two men shouting. My partner ran away. I stayed rooted to the spot, crying."

Guests at the hostel have the opportunity, if they wish, to fill out a report of any ghostly experience in the building. Surprisingly, a number of travellers take the time to share their experiences.

Guests and visitors of the hostel can tour the gallows. The hangman's noose still swings from the rafter inside.

On April 8, 2004, a guest wrote this, "We were going up to the seventh floor to see this noose thing (gallows). My three friends and I suddenly heard 'help me, help me.' We freaked. We were not expecting this. We still had three more nights left here. We hadn't even spent our first night yet. I was so excited."

On July 19, 2004, Matt and a friend stayed overnight at the hostel. Matt wrote, "Last night at about 3:30 p.m. I was walking past death row with my friend. I was commenting on how stupid I thought Whelan was for busting a cap (shooting a bullet) in McGee's ass, instead of poisoning him. Then I got this really creepy vibe shortly thereafter. Then all of a sudden, I got a nose bleed.

"Later the two of us went through death row with two-way radios to talk to our other roommate. As soon as we opened the door to death row my radio started to make a howling sound, which got louder the closer we got to cell 4. Creepy as hell!"

In January 2005 Anne wrote, "I came back to the hostel at 3:00 a.m.; I was neither drunk nor hallucinating. I was alone in the lobby typing an email when I heard ghosts wailing in the wall behind me (behind the front desk). It was very clear and unmistakable (just like what you would hear in a horror movie). The rest of the morning didn't get less scary either. I went to my jail cell on floor four, too scared to use the bathrooms. On this floor, earlier that day, I had heard of a story that had happened just the week before. An Australian school teacher had been in the bathrooms on floor four. She saw a woman wearing only a blanket that went over her head. When the woman turned around, the teacher saw that this woman had no face. Needless to say, after hearing the ghosts in the lobby, I was expecting to see this faceless woman in the fourth floor bathroom.

"Too scared, I went to the fifth floor bathroom. As soon as I went into the bathroom, the pipes started to bang very loudly and mysteriously stopped banging when I left the bathroom. The same thing happened when I hurried up to use the bathroom on the seventh floor."

On August 12, 2005, Holly encountered an apparition on death row. She stated, "I was walking down death row when I swear I saw someone in a long black cloak. When I walked by they waved and said, 'hi there' in a very squawky voice. It was in the cell where they say all the creepy stuff happens. It really creeped me out."

Greg is so keen to develop more interactive activities with the spirits in the building that, starting in July 2007, medium Connie Adams from the Merrickville Psychics Parlour began conducting séances at night on death row. According to Greg, "Connie also feels the spirits who come around the participants, as well as the spirits that live in the building."

In April 2005 she held the first séance, just with the hostel staff. Greg participated. "She got the staff so emotionally charged that some people began to cry in the intense atmosphere. Now I get goose bumps every time I go up to death row."

What does Connie Adams think about all this?

"It was the first time I had ever been in the building when I held the séance on death row last October. During the séance I got a sensation that the jail keeper was coming up the stairs. I could hear his keys rattling. I can always see and sense spirits coming. In the case of this phantom, I could see about 20 rats racing ahead of him. I could see the participants begin to squirm once the rats arrived. Then he stepped forth and the temperature dropped.

Exterior shot of Carleton Gaol.

"I noticed that not one member of the group would sit in front of the second cell near the gallows. Something was going on with the person who was seated in the corner of the room by the steel door. I could clearly see a spirit swiping or brushing at the persons arm. The participant could actually feel someone grabbing at them. I described this spirit as looking like the movie character Hannibal Lecter. I could see it coming near to the participant's neck.

"Later that night, after I went to bed, I began to dream about the jail. I was quite lucid and saw myself checking the energy and closing all the doors to protect everyone from harm. I then saw myself in the basement of the jail. I was a young lady wearing a bonnet and an old-fashioned hooped dress. Next, this lecherous spirit appeared again in front of me. He was testing me. He had such bad teeth and breath. I knew then that everyone was safe from him."

I asked Connie to explain what she experiences when she conducts a séance.

"I can often see a person's past, present, and even their future. I can name all their family members." Then she mentioned seeing orbs of light. I asked her to explain what she thinks an orb of light represents.

"I see orbs in the air. These orbs are energy forces that come from different dimensions. Usually I see sparks in the air first and then one orb will appear. This first orb is a scout for the others. They are there to make sure it is safe for the others to come. Then others will follow arrive. These orbs are either coloured or translucent. They appear for a reason. The yellow-coloured orbs are there for health related issues. For example, they will travel around the person and then go inside them. They are there to cleanse and heal a person. This is a very healing experience at a soul level."

There is no question that Connie's séances will become a popular event at the Ottawa Jail Hostel.

It would seem that there is more going on here now than there was in 1997. Recently, a couple, who were visiting Ottawa, decided to take the ghost tour of the jail. During the tour the man entered a jail cell and asked his partner to take a picture of him behind bars. Later in the evening when they went to review the pictures they were shocked to discover the figure of a person standing behind the man in the jail-cell photograph. They made a copy of the picture which now hangs on the wall by the main desk.

If you need a room in Ottawa for the night you might consider the Ottawa Jail Hostel, but be sure to keep your eye on your clothes, your watch, and your nerves! And remember, this is not for the faint-hearted!

The Bermuda Triangle of the Great Lakes

~ Kingston and Picton ~

A PLACE MARKED BY UNEXPLAINED FORCES CAN BE FOUND OUT ON THE open waters of Lake Ontario. Some people refuse to believe it exists. Others light candles and pray.

For the past two hundred years and maybe more, ships, planes, and people have mysteriously vanished into thin air. Unusual objects and lights can be seen there, streaking across the sky. Known to sailors and others as a mysterious place of dread, it was named "The Marysburgh Vortex" in 1980 by Hugh Cochrane in his book, *Gateway to Oblivion*.

Hugh Cochrane's account begins in 1883 when the *Quinlan* sailed out of Oswego harbour loaded with coal. She was headed on a course straight through the middle of what is now called the Marysburgh Vortex. No one could have foreseen the bizarre events that awaited the ship and her crew. Her fate, it seemed, was sealed the moment she was out in open water.

The *Quinlan* sailed into a fog bank. It was greedily engulfed in that misty blanket of moisture. Plummeting temperatures precipitated ice crystals on the deck and the railings and a driving snow was soon to follow. The crew was unable to keep up with clearing the deck and the churning waters tossed the ship and slammed its wooden structure. The crew held on for dear life.

The *Quinlan* was gripped and steered by some unknown force through the Marysburgh Vortex. Witnesses on land watched as her masts were snapped and her hull was split. Eventually she was tossed on the rocks near shore. A few crewmen were rescued, but most of them, tangled in rigging or injured, were pulled with the ship back into the lake, never to be seen again. The handful of survivors agreed that the ship had been gripped by an "odd attraction."

In 1889 the *Armenia*, a tall-masted ship, sailed out of Kingston harbour at the end of May. The crew and captain were in search of the mysterious disappearance of another vessel, *Bavaria*.

Nine miles south of the Main Duck Islands the crew spotted the *Bavaria*, sitting upright on a small shoal.

As soon as the *Armenia* was within hailing distance, the crew called out — and were answered by silence. The solemn mood was broken only by the creaking of her timbers as the waters of Lake Ontario nudged her from side to side.

Something was very strange. As the captain and crew drew alongside, their suspicions were confirmed. The *Bavaria* was a ghost ship. The crew had completely disappeared without a single trace. Although a small amount of water was found to be in her hold, the ship was still seaworthy. A small repair job, visible on the deck, had been set aside, as though the seaman had been suddenly interrupted.

What mysterious force had beset the crew of the *Bavaria*? Searchers discovered a batch of freshly baked bread in the galley oven. The captain's papers were on his desk along with a box containing a large quantity of money. It had been collected from the cargo recently delivered to American ports. Who would have left the money behind?

In one cabin a canary still chirped in its cage. It was ironic that the only survivor of such a mystery could not tell the tale.

The seamen did discover that one lifeboat was missing. Some men thought an explanation might still be found. The search continued.

On the return of the *Armenia* to Kingston, news of a ghost ship spread throughout the city. People speculated, but what was even more significant, they began to recall earlier days when others had set sail, never to return. Unnatural happenings in this region of water on Lake Ontario became a subject of much conversation.

Several days later it was reported by the captain of another vessel that there had been a storm at the time. They had sighted a lifeboat with two motionless figures at the oars shortly thereafter but repeated attempts to pull alongside failed. Each time the lifeboat was drawn away. No matter how the captain manoeuvred his vessel, the lifeboat remained out of reach. Eventually, the lifeboat disappeared into a thick fog and was never seen again. The two men in the boat had simply stared blankly and made no effort to be saved.

A lighthouse keeper also reported seeing two men adrift in a boat. He, too, attempted to save the men, but to no avail. According to him, each time he had the boat within his grasp he failed to snag it. He also reported that the men made no sound or attempt to be saved.

It remains a mystery.

In June 1900 the ship *Picton*, heavily laden with coal, sailed on course for the Marysburgh Vortex. Following in close proximity were the ships *Minnes* and *Acadia*, the crews of which rubbed their eyes in disbelief. The *Picton* had vanished before their very eyes.

While the men prayed silently, the other ships entered the vortex. They searched for hours, to no avail. There were no signs of wreckage, no signs of survivors. They concluded that the *Picton* had somehow sailed into the unknown.

When they reached port on the Canadian side, the crews shared their stories with others. Many listeners nodded their heads as if acknowledging what was already understood: the Marysburgh Vortex was a place where people and ships could vanish without a trace.

Others still hoped for a sign of wreckage or of a lone survivor. A few days later a clue surfaced at Sackets Harbour just a few miles northeast of where the *Picton* was last seen. The young son of a local fisherman spotted a bottle floating in the water just off the harbour. He borrowed his father's boat and rowed out to get it. To his amazement he discovered a message from Captain Sidley in the bottle. Captain Sidley, of the missing *Picton*! The news of such a find became the talk of the district.

What was that message?

Sidley had written that he had lashed himself to his son in order that they could be found together. That was the extent of his hurried note.

Certainly the existence of such a note indicated that the captain and his son did not die suddenly but had experienced some sort of chaos. Some researchers believe the *Picton* entered a doorway to another dimension.

The next autumn, 1915, at the end of the shipping season, the *F.C. Barnes* set sail along the north shore of Lake Ontario headed for Kingston. Witnesses later remarked that while watching the ship from shore it seemed to disappear into a cloud of mist. Once again, this occurrence was at the edge of the Marysburgh Vortex.

When the mist dissipated, the tug was no longer visible. Although a search party scoured the waters, no debris was ever found to explain its disappearance. Authorities listed the disappearance of the *F.C. Barnes* as "unexplained."

The eeriest story on record is the simple but bizarre story of Captain George Donner. On April 28, 1937, Captain Donner and his crew sailed down the middle of Lake Ontario. At 10:15 p.m. the captain ordered the second mate to notify him when they neared their destination and then he retired to his cabin.

A few hours later the second mate knocked at the captain's door. There was no answer. He continued to knock. Something was wrong. He opened the cabin door. No one was there. The crew searched the entire ship. Captain Donner had vanished. Some of the crew testified that they had seen him enter his cabin. Others had heard him moving about in his quarters.

The authorities in port launched a thorough investigation. Nothing turned up. Was it possible that the captain fell overboard? This was quickly discounted since the trip was calm and an experienced sailor like Donner would not have fallen overboard.

Although the authorities alerted all vessels to watch for his body, nothing ever surfaced. Another unsolved mystery.

David Childress, in his book entitled, *Anti-Gravity & the World Grid*, described the existence of an Earth Grid or "crystalline Earth" in the Marysburgh Vortex.

According to Childress, "This Earth Grid is comprised of geometrical flow lines of gravity in the structure of the Earth itself."

Richard Lefors Clark made reference to this in an article called "Earth Grid, Human Levitation & Gravity Anomalies." He states, "The pyramids and ley lines are on the power transfer lines of the natural Earth gravity Grid all over the world. The Earth Grid is comprised of the geometrical flow lines of gravity energy in the structure of the Earth itself.

"While the subject of the Earth Grid has been covered in a considerable number of publications, one point in the Grid, marked by a long and strange history at the eastern tip of Lake Ontario is worth special mention."

David Childress also refers to the significant number of aircraft and ship incidents in the Lake Ontario Earth Grid area known as "The Other Bermuda Triangle" and "The Gateway to Oblivion on the eastern end of Lake Ontario."

Clark referred to a project started in 1950 by the National Research Council (NRC) of Canada and the United States Army to investigate the magnetic anomalies and possible magnetic utility of this area. Officials call it "Project Magnet." Was it top secret? Perhaps.

Project Magnet was the first official government research program involving the Earth Grid System. Wilbert Smith, a Canadian communications engineer for the Department of Transportation, directed the project. Smith and a team of scientists did find something. However, as Richard Clark explained, "Project Magnet was terminated."

Wilbert Smith was born in Lethbridge, Alberta in 1910. According to journalist Paul McManus in an article entitled "Project Magnet," "Smith graduated from the University of British Columbia, with degrees in electrical engineering and worked as the chief engineer for radio station CJOR in Vancouver. By 1939 Smith was working for the federal Department of Transportation designing Canada's wartime monitoring systems."

McManus added, "In 1950 Smith attended a North America Radio Broadcast Association conference in Washington, DC, where he became further convinced of the existence of UFO's, and that they used magnetic forces to operate."

Smith described what happened at the conference. "In 1950 I was attending a rather slow-moving broadcasting conference in Washington, DC, and having some free time on my hands, I circulated around asking a few questions about flying saucers, which stirred up a hornet's nest. I found that the United States government had a highly classified project set up to study them, so I reasoned that with so much smoke maybe I should look for the fire."

Upon his return to Ottawa, Smith met with Dr. Omond Solandt, chairman of the Canadian Defence Research Board. Solandt agreed to provide laboratory space, equipment, and personnel for research into geo-magnetism.

McManus stated, "In his project proposal of November 21, 1950, Smith outlined seven areas of geo-magnetic research. UFO research was not mentioned. Commander C.P. Edwards, Deputy Minister of Transport for Air Services, accepted the proposal. The project, named Magnet, was department classified, as there was a potential to create new technologies with unknown potential."

By 1953 Project Magnet moved into the Department of Transport facilities at Shirley's Bay, just upstream of Ottawa, on the Ottawa River. Some of his research equipment included a magnetometer, a gamma-ray detector, a powerful radio receiver, and a gravimeter, in order to measure gravity fields in the atmosphere.

Wilbert Smith described Project Magnet in these terms. "Project Magnet was authorized in December 1950, following my request to the Canadian department of Transport for permission to make use of the Departments' laboratory and field facilities in a study of unidentified flying objects and physical principals which might appear to be involved."

In an article entitled "We are Not Alone," Wilbert Smith truly described his beliefs and findings. "Our universe is a very large place. The universe is also incredibly old. Maybe the universe doesn't even have an age, that it is eternal and ever passing through the cycle of energy to matter and matter to energy.

"It is only reasonable to speculate that somewhere else in the vastness of space and the eternity of time, other intelligent life could have blossomed forth. Since we have made such rapid progress toward space travel in such a short time, a differential of only a few hundred or at the most a few thousand years between the development on some other planet and ours could easily have resulted in a race capable of doing right now what we plan to do in the future. In fact, intelligent races might even set about accelerating environmental conditions to their liking, seeding and stocking planets with appropriate life forms, and watching over them as they develop."

Smith then addressed the UFO sightings.

"Thousands of people have seen lights and apparently solid objects in the sky that behaved as no light or object normally seen in the sky ought to behave. Thousands have seen these objects under circumstances, which enabled them to say definitely what they were not, even though they were not able to say what they were. Reliable photographs and movies have been taken, and bits of 'hardware' collected which cannot be explained away without challenging the integrity of a great many cases, and there is quite a bit of evidence of physical contact with these strange craft."

Smith summarized by stating, "There is virtually no doubt that alien craft are visiting this Earth, and that the beings who operate them are very much like us, probably our distant relatives."

By 1953 the press became suspicious of Smith's work. Word leaked out that he and his team were doing UFO research. Questions were soon asked of the Department of Transport. Paul McManus stated, "Denials were made, but it became obvious that something unusual was under way.

On August 8, 1954, "contact" was made at 3:01 p.m. The gravimeter results, recorded on graph paper, showed a very large and unexplainable deflection and the researchers rushed outside to have a look. All they saw was dense cloud cover.

Two days later the Department of Transport issued a press release admitting they had been performing UFO research for three-and-a-half years.

Smith stated what happened next. "When the Project Magnet report was made and permission sought to extend the scope of the investigations through federal support, the decision was finally made in 1954 that this would not be advisable in the face of the publicity from which the whole project had suffered."

The conclusions reached by Project Magnet and contained in the official report were based on rigid statistical analysis of sightings and were as follows:

There is a 91 percent probability that at least some of the sightings were of real objects of unknown origin.

There is about a 60 percent probability that these objects are alien vehicles.

In 1961 Smith was involved in an interview with television station CJOH. During the session he was asked if he believed that flying saucers were real.

Smith replied, "Yes. I am convinced that they are just as real and tangible as most things we deal with in our everyday lives."

"Next question, Have you, yourself, actually handled any material believed to be from a flying saucer?"

Smith, "If by that, you mean material substance showing evidence of fabrication through intelligent effort and not originating on this planet, I have."

During the interview Smith never used the word UFO. He knew from the very beginning that the phenomena he was studying and tracking was extraterrestrial.

According to Wilbert's son, Jim Smith, just prior to his father's death in 1962 his father called him in, and told Jim that he had in fact seen the alien bodies from a crash, and had been shown the crashed remains of a flying saucer outside Washington D.C while conducting the official Canadian investigation.

Smith did reveal that there were sometimes mobile gravity anomalies all over the Lake Ontario area. He especially noted areas of "reduced binding" in the atmosphere above the lake. He described the areas as "pillar-like columns a thousand feet up in the atmosphere." Some of these invisible, mysterious columns appear to change location.

One phenomenon that might play a role in the unexplained events in the Marysburgh Vortex is the number of magnetic anomalies. According to Smith there are no fewer than 14 of these magnetic anomalies — areas of strong local magnetic disturbance — plainly marked on present-day navigation charts. The majority of these locations are clustered in the eastern end of Lake Ontario.

The Marysburgh Vortex was also one area where Smith conducted a number of investigations into UFO sightings. There had been another earlier discovery here that may have the same origins but also has some folkloric aspects. In 1804, Captain Charles Selleck and his crew of the *Lady Murray* detected something on the surface of the water during a crossing of Lake Ontario. It seemed that in one small area the wave movement was different. The ship was stopped and a lifeboat was lowered over the side. He and some crew members rowed to the area to investigate.

What they found was a gigantic stone monolith just three feet (one metre) beneath the surface. It measured 40 feet (over ten metres) square. Sounding it revealed a sheer drop on all sides of approximately 300 feet (less than 100 metres) straight down.

The captain entered his findings in his logbook; this object was a major navigational hazard and others would need that information. Curious seekers sailed out to poke and prod this immense monolith for many months to follow. Among the visitors to the site was Captain Thomas Paxton of the government schooner *Speedy*. No one knew what this foreshadowed for Captain Paxton. An event near the village of Port Perry on Lake Scugog would precipitate this strange incident.

In 1806 the Farewell family opened a trading post for barter with the Native peoples on Washburn's Island on Lake Scugog. One day the Farewells left their agent, John Sharp, in charge of the post. When they returned, they found him dead. It was alleged that a Native named Ogetonicut had done the deed to avenge the murder, by a white man, of his brother, Whistling Duck. Ogetonicut was arrested and after a preliminary hearing it was decided that the trial would be held at the Newcastle courthouse.

Newcastle was the new district town planned for Northumberland and Durham to be located at Presqu'ile. The murder had been committed in that judicial district. Ogetonicut was taken first to York, now Toronto, to await transportation to Presqu'ile. A government schooner named the *Speedy* was chartered in October to take those who needed to be present at the trial down the lake. Judge Thomas Cochrane, court officials, and a selected group of dignitaries were to officiate.

The *Speedy* had two alternate captains. One was Thomas Paxton and the other was James Richardson. Apparently Richardson had some forewarning concerning the trip, his intuition told him not to go. There was danger. He attempted to change the minds of the officials. Even the witnesses refused to board. Paxton, however, was ordered to do the job.

According to local lore, Ogetonicut's mother travelled from Lake Scugog to the shores of Lake Ontario near Oshawa to watch for the *Speedy*.

When she caught sight of the vessel, and in the knowledge that her son was on board, she began to chant against those who had taken him away.

That evening a violent storm struck. By midnight, enormous waves crashed the shore. The *Speedy* was being pursued by a deadly gale. Captain Paxton, for some unknown reason, never sought the shelter of the harbours he passed in the night. Instead, the ship steered straight for Presqu'ile Bay.

As the ship neared its destination, locals lit bonfires to help direct the ship into harbour, but the *Speedy* seemed to be on a different course. Hugh Cochrane elaborated, "The captain paid them no heed. Nor did he appear to have control of his vessel, for her course seemed unerring. As if drawn by a huge magnet, the ship headed directly for the area of the monolith, then was lost from sight as the storm closed over the scene."

That was the last time anyone saw the *Speedy*.

The ship had simply disappeared. The next day searchers sailed out to the area of the monolith hoping to find either survivors or wreckage of the ship. They were shocked when they dragged the lake and found nothing. Even the stone monolith was gone. There was no longer a three hundred foot depth of water; instead, it was shallow and sandy.

No wreckage and no survivors of the *Speedy* were ever found.

Janet Kellough is a seventh generation Prince Edward County resident. She knows about the existence of the Marysburgh Vortex. "When you're in a recreational boat your compass doesn't work out there. I know a pilot who was flying out over the middle of the vortex when he encountered a strange phenomenon. It was like a giant hand reached out and flipped his plane over. Then a sudden force righted the craft. People also report seeing strange lights out over these waters."

Dave Whatton has lived in Prince Edward County for the past 54 years. He is a local historian who is knowledgeable concerning these events and who has theories about this mysterious area in Ontario. I asked David to share his views.

"I will say that many of the doomed sailors on the vessels that disappeared undoubtedly experienced some form of shock, which can separate various aspects of the Etheric body from the other body layers. This results in emotionally charged energy fragments that loop. We know them as 'ghosts.' They are quite akin to an endless loop video of a few seconds duration. The figure appears, does its thing, then disappears, only to repeat the scene any number of times.

"This repeating pattern has been noted throughout the world, and certainly has manifested itself in this area. I recognize that the phenomenon is truly real to the perceiver and that certain individuals are more able to receive this sensory-based communication than others.

"I live in the so-called Marysburgh Vortex. It is a quiet, rural area populated by a mixture of farm folk, fisher folk, and city escapists.

"The specific area referred to by some as the Marysburgh Vortex is in the extreme southeastern sector of Prince Edward County, bounded by water on three sides with no more than two miles of land separating an arm of inland sea, namely Prince Edward Bay, from Lake Ontario proper.

"The Marysburgh Vortex is more than just a mysterious place where people, ships and planes go missing, it is a sacred territory emitting a strong atmosphere of mysticism and of healing qualities."

As to the spirituality of the area, David points out that shamans of various Native cultures spanning thousands of years have treated this area as sacred. The Hopewell/Adena (circa 300 B.C.) not only settled in this spot for several hundred years but built their Mounds here as well. "Two thousand years later, the island of Waupoos was named after a Cayuga holy man. The ancients knew that this area was special and I concur."

If you plan to sail in The Marysburgh Vortex or even to pay a visit, keep your eyes peeled for the unusual — lights, mists, and vanishing objects; keep your ears keened and listening for unexplained cries in the night and keep your mind and other senses tuned and open. Light your candles; and say your prayers. The mystery continues.

The Ghost of Tom Thomson

~ Canoe Lake in Algonquin Park ~

WHEN A WOMAN OR MAN IS MURDERED THEIR SOUL OFTEN REMAINS the prisoner of the circumstance. They remain on in the vicinity of the crime. For nearly a century, the death of Tom Thomson on Canoe Lake in 1917 has remained a mystery. Was it accidental drowning or was it murder? The existence of his spirit on Canoe Lake could support the theory of murder. You be the judge.

Tom Thomson was born in Claremont, Ontario, on August 4, 1877. At the age of two months, his parents, along with his six brothers and sisters, moved to the town of Leith near Owen Sound on Georgian Bay.

As a young boy he thoroughly enjoyed the outdoors, fishing in the bay, swimming, and boating. Tom had an ear for music and played the violin, mandolin, and coronet. He was also fascinated by birds and the colour of leaves in the autumn and flowers in the spring. According to his brother, George, he paid keen attention to the seasonal movements of animals. As a teenager he was strongly-built and stood almost six feet

Artist Doug Dunford captured this ghostly photograph of Tom Thomson in the morning mist on Canoe Lake before the canoeist disappeared before his very eyes.

(two metres). Judge Little, author of *The Tom Thomson Mystery*, adds, "Conversely he couldn't find satisfaction in study; he neither finished high school nor completed a machinists' apprenticeship started in his late teens at Owen Sound. He also attempted, but never completed, a business course at Chatham."

It was in 1901 at the age of 24 that Tom took his first step toward a career in art. He followed his brothers, George and Henry, to Seattle and there joined a commercial art studio where George had begun a year earlier. There Tom explored the territory of his imagination; there he began experimenting with crayon and then watercolour sketches. Some mention has been given to an unsuccessful romance with a woman in Seattle, which fostered his return to Toronto in 1905. There he found employment with a commercial art firm.

In 1911 he acquired a new job with the firm of Grip Limited. It was here that he made contact with other kindred spirits — J.E.H. MacDonald, Arthur Lismer, Fred Varley, Tom MacLean, A.Y. Jackson, and Frank Carmichael. Now 34 years old, Tom had begun to do sketches and oil paintings around Toronto near the Don Valley, Rosedale Ravine, Scarlet Road, Old Mill, and Lambton.

Given Thomson's aptitude for fishing, it remains unclear why a length of fishing line was wrapped 16 or 17 times around Tom's left ankle at the time of his death.

In early 1912 Tom made his first trek to picturesque Canoe Lake in Algonquin Park. Between 1913 and 1917 he painted there from spring break-up until late fall. The majority of his works were inspired here, including "Northern River," "West Wind," "Spring Ice," "Jack Pine," and "Northern Lights." He painted 24 major canvasses and made more than 300 sketches.

Judge William T. Little quoted park ranger Mark Robinson, who first met Thomson in the spring of 1912, in his book, "One evening as I went to Canoe Lake, a couple of other rangers had joined me. It was quite routine in those days for park rangers to inspect all newcomers coming into the park because poaching was a major offense and a common occurrence in the park. As the train came in and drew to a stop, a tall fine-looking man with a packsack on his back stepped off the train. The stranger inquired where he could find a place to stay, and where he could get a good bed and good eats. I explained to him that the Algonquin Hotel was a short distance away and Mowat Lodge was nearby. A man by the name of Fraser served good meals there and had excellent beds. Tom said that was the place for him."

Mowat Lodge became his home away from home. In the ensuing years Tom lived with the Frasers as if one of the family. He even designed a cover for the Frasers' booklet to announce Mowat Lodge. Tom was, nevertheless, a loner, and often canoed out into the lake to disappear for days on end, painting and fishing to his heart's content. He was an amiable man with rugged, lean, muscular good looks. Tom was well-liked by most who met him and enjoyed the company of others at the many parties in the area.

Mark Robinson points out that Tom earned his way in the park by purchasing a guide license, and subsequently led parties of fishermen through the park. He often tented on the east side of Canoe Lake, opposite Mowat Landing, just north of Hayhurst's Point.

In April 1917 Tom arrived at Canoe Lake for the last time. On July 7 of that year Tom and a number of local cottage residents met at George Rowe's cabin for some merriment. Drinking at these social events usually led to storytelling. The topic of the war arose and Tom spoke of his determination to join up as a fire ranger. His earlier attempts to join had been thwarted because of his flat feet. That night Martin Blecher, who was considered to have a bad temperament only exacerbated by heavy drinking, arrived at the party.

Judge Little wrote, "One young American cottager in particular, Martin Blecher, who was of German background, was most outspoken regarding the progress of the war and his forecast of ultimate German supremacy. During the early summer Tom and Martin seemed to share a

Few photographs exist of Winnie Trainor. Even her home in Huntsville was torn down shortly after her death. Winnie is seen here on the left.

mutual dislike. These two men, during this Saturday evening, were actually prevented from coming to blows only by the good-natured efforts of the guides. On leaving the cabin before midnight, Blecher hurled a final threat, 'Don't get in my way if you know what's good for you.'"

A love triangle can be a source of great pain and jealousy. Secret love is even more entangling and complex. Winnie Trainor was, by all

As an expert outdoorsman, fishing was a passion of Tom Thomson's.

accounts, a beautiful, mysterious woman. Hidden to most, Winnie and Tom shared a secret love. Judge Little said, "Not until Miss Trainor's death in 1962 has it been known authoritatively that Thomson intended to marry her. Did Martin Blecher resent Tom's visits to Winnie Trainor, just next door to him, during those long summer evenings? Did Tom resent Martin's presence so close to Miss Trainor's cottage?"

Terence Trainor McCormick, the nephew and beneficiary of Miss Trainor's estate, once stated about the letters written between Winnie and Tom, "… the correspondence gave undisputable evidence that Tom and my Aunt were engaged to be married." Their covenant remains a secret known only to them.

It was a rather dull morning and wet on Sunday, July 8, 1917. Shannon Fraser and Tom threw a line in the water at the dam between Joe and Canoe Lakes. Mark Robinson caught sight of the men returning. Tom waved to Mark and called, "Howdy, Mark." Mark acknowledged the greeting. It would be the last time he ever saw Tom alive.

Tom returned to his quarters where he gathered up his tackle box and a loaf of bread and some bacon from Mowat Lodge. He bid farewell to Shannon as his canoe cut a path across the waters of Canoe Lake. Shannon watched Tom disappear past Little Wapomeo Island only one and a half kilometres (one mile) away.

The following day Martin Blecher casually remarked to some guests at Mowat Lodge that he had spotted an upturned canoe between Little and Big Wapomeo Islands. Apparently, he and his sister had not stopped, but continued on for an afternoon fishing excursion. On their return trip the canoe had disappeared.

No one seemed too concerned about such a report. It was a strange reaction by such a small community of residents who all knew the boats on the lake. Judge Little adds, "Furthermore, Canoe Lake residents considered it strange that Martin Blecher could not have recognized Thomson's grey-green canoe with a metal strip on the keel side; it was known to everyone on Canoe Lake at the time."

Charlie Scrim found the craft the following morning behind Big Wapomeo Island. Mark Robinson said, "Contrary to some people who may tell you the canoe was floating right side up, there was none of his equipment in the canoe, except his portaging paddle, which was lashed in position for carrying, and the ground sheet with bread and bacon in the bow section. There were no fishing poles, no gear; even his small axe was gone."

Robinson immediately reported to Park Superintendent Bartlett who authorized a search. Tom's brother George was contacted. He arrived at Canoe Lake on July 12. Dynamite was exploded in the lake without the desired results — no body surfaced.

The sharp eyes and minds of guides George Rowe and Charlie Scrim noted that Tom's own working paddle was missing. Especially strange was how the portaging paddle was lashed in a position to portage. It had been knotted in a most unorthodox way. Only an inexperienced canoeist would fashion such a knot. Thomson was an expert canoeist and outdoorsman.

On July 14 George Thomson gathered up a number of Tom's sketches and caught the train back to New York. He felt there was little he could do.

On the morning of July 15, 1917, Dr. G.W. Howland spotted something lying low in the water by Hayhurst Point on the east shore of Canoe Lake. At first he thought it was a loon. At the same time George

Rowe and Lowrie Dickson were paddling down the middle of the lake when they saw the doctor hailing them. The canoeists aimed for the object. It was Tom. He was dead.

They towed the body to a campsite on Big Wapomeo, approximately 100 yards (300 metres) ahead. There at Big Wap, a campout halfway down the west side of the lake, they tied the body to tree roots in a shallow. The guides then notified Dr. Howland and Mark Robinson who contacted Superintendent Bartlett.

Dr. A.E. Ranney, a coroner living in North Bay, was notified. He did not arrive on the train the next day. Robinson was frantic and informed his Superintendent that something needed to be done with the body. It was not right to leave it in the blazing sun. The Superintendent informed Mark to have Dr. Howland examine the body. Dr. Howland was a Toronto medical doctor and a professor of neurology at the University of Toronto who was vacationing on Wapomeo Island. Mark then ordered a casket and rough box for the burial.

On the morning of July 17 Dr. Howland examined the deceased. Mark helped to remove a length of fishing line that was wrapped 16 or 17 times around Tom's left ankle. That was odd. There was no water in the lungs. Across the left temple was a mark that looked as though he had been struck with the edge of a paddle. The doctor's report read: "A bruise on left temple the size of four inches long, no other sign of external marks visible on body, air issuing from mouth, some bleeding from right ear. Cause of death, drowning."

Tom was placed in a casket and moved to the mainland for a hurried funeral. A small congregation of Canoe Lake residents and guides, including Miss Trainor, witnessed the burial at Canoe Lake Cemetery. Miss Trainor caught the evening train for Huntsville. She would never again greet her lover by the water's edge. Or would she?

A short time later a telegram arrived to the attention of Shannon Fraser. It was a request by Mr. H.W. Churchill, a Huntsville undertaker, to exhume the body. Apparently the family had requested that Tom be interred near the family home at Leith, Ontario. At 8:00 p.m. Fraser met the eastbound train at Canoe Lake Station. Churchill got off the train wearing a dark suit, and bowler hat. He informed Fraser that he had a metal casket with him and asked that Fraser give him a hand to put it on his wagon.

The cross marks the original gravesite of Tom Thomson. It was here that Judge Little and his friends uncovered a body in a grave alleged to be empty.

With a call to the horses they were off. Fraser was stunned to learn that Churchill was going to remove the body that very night. It all seemed very strange. Fraser remarked that he couldn't get any help until the next day.

Judge Little quoted the following conversation, "The undertaker replied, 'I don't need any help, just get me a good digging shovel, a lantern and a crow bar and I'll do the rest.'"

"'Here we are,' announced Shannon. 'Do you still want to do this job tonight without any help?'"

"'Just pick me up about midnight and I'll be ready,' replied the undertaker."

Fraser returned at midnight to give Churchill a hand to place the casket on the rear baggage floor of the coach and transport the body to the train station. Judge Little highlights an oddity that occurred, "Fraser was to comment a number of times later, 'It just didn't impress me the weight was distributed the way it should be with a body in it.'"

Judge Little also documented Mark Robinson's comments, "The Superintendent called me up and said, 'Go down to the cemetery and if they haven't filled the grave in, fill it in.' I went down. Now, in one

Judge Little had to see for himself if Tom Thomson was still buried at Canoe Lake. From left to right: Leonard Gibson, William T. Little, W.J. Eastaugh, and Frank Braught starting to dig. To their amazement, they discovered a body in Thomson's grave.

corner of the grave was a hole I wouldn't say it would be more than 20 inches and about a depth of 18 inches. God forgive me if I'm wrong but I still think Thomson's body is over there (Mark pointed to the hillside gravesite where Tom was originally interred)."

In the 1950s Judge Little and three other men, Jack Eastaugh, Leonard Gibson, and Frank Braught decided to investigate the Thomson mystery themselves. They firmly believed Tom was still buried in the Canoe Lake

Cemetery. The Judge was convinced he had been murdered. Armed with shovels and axes the men began to clear the underbrush. At six feet (two metres) they found nothing. Then Jack called out from beside a spruce tree. There were depressions three feet (one metre) wide in the ground. They began to dig. They struck pay dirt. The shovel found the remains of a rough pine box. No name was inscribed on the box. There was no evidence of metal remnants, such as buttons, belt buckle, shoe nails nor clothing.

Judge Little described the scene, "We saw parts of the casket lining and what appeared to be possibly a cotton or light canvas shroud. We recalled that, after Tom's examination by Dr. Howland, the body was immediately placed in a casket wrapped only in a shroud due to the removal of clothes related to the advanced state of decomposition of the body. We also discovered a hole in the temple region of the skull which coincided with the region indicated at both the inquest and in Mark Robinson's observations of a blow to the temple."

A short time later Dr. Henry Ebbs and Dr. Noble Sharpe of the Ontario Provincial Criminal Laboratory arrived at Canoe Lake. They gathered the skeletal remains and photographed the skull with its puncture at the temple.'

Dr. Sharpe later concluded, "The bones were definitely male. Calculations from humerus, femur, and tibia gave an estimated height of five feet and eight inches. These bones suggested also a robust, well-muscled person."

Professor J.C.B Grant, of the Department of Anthropology, University of Toronto, was asked for his opinion. He stated, "The skeleton was of a male, strong, height five feet and eight inches plus or minus two inches, age in late 20s and of Mongolian type, either Indian or nearly full-breed Indian."

Further studies were made of the skull, including x-rays. According to Judge Little, "X-ray of the skull before emptying out the sand showed no bullet in the skull and none found in the sand after emptying. The hole in the left temple region is nearly three-quarters of an inch (less than two centimetres) in diameter. The inner plate opening is slightly wider showing a slight beveling. No radiating fractures were seen in x-ray. There was no injury on the inner table of the skull opposite the hole where a bullet would impinge. The orbital plate and nasal bones were so intact that no bullet could have escaped from the skull." Therefore, the hole in the temple was not the result of a bullet wound.

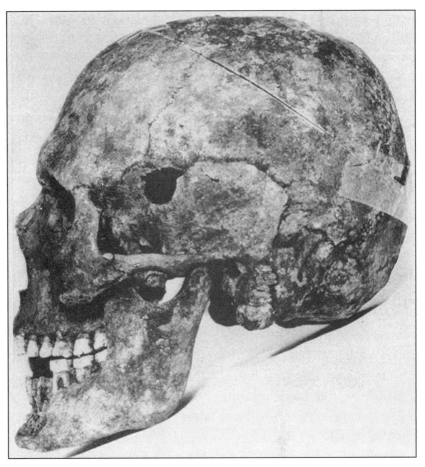

The skull removed from Thomson's grave indicates a hole in the temple coinciding with the injury sustained by the artist.

Professor Eric Linnell of the Department of Neuropathology concluded, "The wound, however, though definitely not due to a bullet, could be caused by a sharp instrument such as a pick, a narrow hammer head." Maybe a paddle?

Judge Little responded to the investigation, "The foot of the grave in which the bones were found was 21 feet (seven metres) due north of the corner of the fence surrounding the two marked graves. This is certainly approximately where Mr. Thomson was buried originally. There is nothing to prove that the opened grave is not the same as Mr. Thomson's and the coffin is just as his was said to be."

Stone commemorating the death of Tom Thomson.

Why so much conflicting information? Did this group of men really dig up the remains of Tom Thomson? There should have been no body at all!

Jane Loftus, the daughter of the late Judge Little, states, "My father always believed the body they found in Canoe Lake Cemetery was that of Tom Thomson."

In 1935 Miss Blodwen Davies, an official of the Saskatchewan Art Board, published a biography of Tom Thomson. It was while doing the research for the book that she investigated his death. She concluded, "I came away from my investigation with the conviction there had been foul play. I tried to get the Ontario Government to open an investigation but they said it had all happened so long ago it was best to leave it alone."

Miss Davies spent the rest of her life pursuing the mystery. She once wrote concerning the testimony at the inquest, "No one remarked that only a living body could be bruised or bleed, or that Thomson's lungs were full with air, not with water."

A questionnaire she used with Mark Robinson is reprinted courtesy of the Archives of Canada, Ottawa:

Question: How deep was the water in which Thomson was found?

Answer: About 30 feet (10 metres).

Question: How far was it from shore?

Answer: 125 yards (120 metres).

Question: Was his fishing rod and line found?

Answer: No.

Question: Do you think it was his own line which was wound around his ankle?

Answer: It might have been his own line but not his regular fishing line.

Question: Did you see a mark on his forehead and if so, what was it like?

Answer: A slight bruise over the eyebrow.

Question: Did the Blechers aid in the search for Thomson?

Answer: They did on the Lake. They did not search in the woods as far as I know.

Question: Did they make any attempt to direct the search?

Answer: No. They were very quiet in every way.

Little added, "Who was it that struck him a blow across the temple — and was it done with the edge of a paddle blade? — that sent the blood spurting from his ear?"

So many of Thomson's friends were puzzled over his death. Many did not believe that he had drowned. Miss Davies adds, "Why did Thomson's body take eight days to rise in a shallow lake in the middle of July? Bodies that have been in warm summer waters usually rise after a couple of days, due to bloating. Could the fishing line bound round the lower left leg have been tied to some weighty object such as a stone?

"If Tom struck his head on rocks after death, how could the body bleed? Bodies do not bruise or bleed after death. This man was not accident prone; he was a canoeist of exceptional skill. The weather and water conditions were calm. It is difficult to believe he just fell out of his canoe and received a severe wound to his head."

In a letter written to Judge Little, from Miss Margaret Howland on May 2, 1969, from Willowdale, Ontario she stated, "My father, the late

Dr. Howland, in subsequent discussion mentioned the fact that there was a possibility that the drowning of Tom Thomson was not accidental.

"This possibility, I think, had been considered at the inquest and his comment was made following it or shortly after rather than many years after the incident as you say."

Tom Thomson has never left Canoe Lake. Speculation says that he was murdered and he was in love. Just ask Mrs. Northway and Canadian artist, Lawren Harris, who resided in the park in the summer of 1931. They believe he appeared on the waters that year.

Judge Little recorded their experience, "It had been a happy day and ever so lazy. At dusk we were coming home, tired, rested, and at peace with the world. It was a tremendously still evening; you could hear the silence against your ear. The hills made strange, statuesque figures against the haunting orange of the western sky, while the first star set its light akindle, as an alter lamp of the universe against the canopy of the afterglow. Even my guide's tales ceased, and through my mind drifted fragments of harmonies as if heard from a far away 'cello.' Suddenly the voice of my guide shattered the silence. 'They're coming out to meet us from the portage.'

"And turning toward the sunset I saw a man kneeling in a canoe that slowly came toward us. 'So they are', I answered. 'I guess we are pretty late.'

"My guide turned from his course in order that we might better meet our herald, now a little less than 100 yards (90 metres) away. I raised my voice and called, and waved my hand, while my guide kept paddling toward the camper. But there was no response, for even as we looked the canoe and its paddler, without warning or sound, vanished into nothingness, and on the undisturbed lake were only our lonely selves and the shrieking of a loon."

Miss Northway added some observations her mother had left out of the story, "As my mother was coming into the bay by the portage, she saw a canoe and a paddler in a yellow shirt. 'They're coming out from the portage to meet us,' said the guide. The man waved and the guide waved back. Then the paddler, canoe and all, completely vanished.

"My father and Mr. Taylor Statten, being practical people, on hearing the tale, insisted it had been a mirage, but Lawren Harris was sure it was the spirit of Tom Thomson. His rationale was that those who depart before their time continue to haunt the lands they loved.

"My mother was inclined to accept Lawren's interpretation, much to my father's disgust. A point that was much discussed, but never settled, was what colour of shirt was Tom wearing when he was drowned?"

For years people have reported seeing a phantom canoeist travelling the waters of Algonquin Park. One moment you see a man paddling a canoe across the way and in the next, he vanishes. Many eye-witness accounts refer to the canoeist as Tom Thomson. One witness to such an event was drawn to paint the experience.

Doug Dunford is a professional artist best known for his ability to capture the symbols of Muskoka life in high realist style. He lives in the Muskokas.

Early in his career he was given one of A.Y. Jackson's easels and one of his old chairs. These were his first connections to the Group of Seven painters, but others followed.

In the summer of 1980 Doug found himself painting a new sign for Algonquin Park. For two weeks he immersed himself in the natural beauty of the park. Doug has always believed, "You have to live the art in the environment where you work."

One evening a social gathering took place at a cottage on Canoe Lake. Doug recalls, "The next morning I decided to go down to the dock. A thick mist was enshrouding Canoe Lake. I just stood on the dock with my camera hanging around my neck, looking. Then I heard this trickling sound like a paddle in the water. Suddenly a person in a canoe emerged from the mist. We made eye contact and then he turned and vanished. For some unknown reason I took his picture just before he turned and disappeared, as abruptly and mystically as he had appeared.

"In that moment I sensed a strange energy. It took me off guard. I have felt that strange feeling before. I don't know why I took the picture and began to second-guess the experience. Had it really happened? Would there be anything on the photograph? I didn't understand why this person had turned so abruptly. Why was someone out on the lake in such fog? Why had he disappeared? I got this strange feeling. Maybe in my own consciousness I made a connection. I do know that I can only connect from my own experience. I knew it was Tom Thomson. I was shocked when the film was developed. There was my phantom canoeist.

"I was drawn to paint the photograph. A good painting depicts what you have experienced. This photograph was a memory of the moment. The painting chooses you. It is always there. It never leaves. One day something triggers it. Within six months after the experience, I painted it. Then I painted over it. I wasn't ready. It didn't feel right.

"When I told people the story they agreed that it indeed could be Tom Thomson. Six or seven years later I did a small watercolour of that dramatic experience on Canoe Lake.

"Then one day, during a show in my gallery, a young man walked in. He was going to school out West. This piece of work, entitled 'The Return of Tom Thomson', was hanging in the show. The man purchased it. About a year later he wrote to me to say that he bought the painting because he had seen the same man in the same canoe in the park. He had felt it had been a ghost himself. He was amazed to see it hanging in my gallery."

On the anniversary of Tom Thomson's death a few people gather on the shore of Canoe Lake to see if he will appear. There is no question, for those who have seen him, that it is Tom.

As for Winnie Trainor, she never married and lived in Huntsville until her death. Jane Loftus pointed out that Miss Trainor would often travel to Canoe Lake and place flowers on the grave of Tom Thomson. Perhaps she never married because she knew he was still there with her. If she saw him and communicated with him, she kept it to herself.

Playwright Stina Nyquist in her Tom Thomson play, *The Shantyman's Daughter*, has Miss Trainor say this about herself, "I'm a slob. I've been one since that summer a long-time ago. I let my hair go. I have soup stains on my blouse, my stockings are rumpled, and so on and so forth. It's not that I'm a slob at heart. I'm not a natural-born slob. I just got that way, bit by bit, since that summer. But once every year, on this day, I dress up. I go to the beauty parlour, I put on this outfit, and this hat — if it's not too windy. I got this dress for a special occasion that didn't happen …"

Gaye Clemson, born and raised in Toronto, now resides in Monterey Bay, California. In the early 1950s her father decided to make Algonquin Park a part of his life and purchased a lease on Canoe Lake. In 1954 her father and mother built a cabin on the leased land.

In the May 2006 issue of *The Muskoka Magazine*, journalist Meaghan Deemeester wrote an article entitled "Canoe Lake," highlighting Clemson and the Thomson Mystery.

The small graveyard overshadowed by an ancient birch stands on a hilltop beyond Canoe Lake. No signs or path marks the way to the cemetery. It remains hidden in the forest.

"Thomson, who was an avid and accomplished canoeist, died on the lake in July 1917. His body was found several days after his upturned canoe was spotted floating on the lake, and despite a four-inch cut/bruise on his left temple, and fishing line tied around his ankle, the authorities quickly deemed his death an accidental drowning.

"However, the residents of Canoe Lake feel differently, believing in most cases that foul play was involved. In fact, in the late 1970s, Clemson's brother found the remains of a paddle stuck in the mud. She says, 'After washing and careful examination of its weather worn condition and the fact that there was a 'cut' out of the blade that looked like it was an exact match to an adult male's temple, he ascertained that it was in fact Toms' long-lost paddle and by inference the long lost murder weapon. It hangs to this day, from our cabin ceiling.'"

Her passion for local history and the tragic death surrounding Tom Thomson led Clemson to create the *Tom Thomson Murder Mystery Game*. According to Deemeester, "In her Murder Mystery Game, Clemson explores some of the conventional theories, mainly the result of other writers' research, surrounding the death. Some of these include:

"Winnie Trainor is pregnant, Thomson doesn't want to marry her; she decides to 'do him in' and make it look like an accident or he commits suicide as a way of getting out of marrying her.

"Shannon Fraser owed him money and Thomson wanted it back in order to get a new suit to marry Trainor. He and Shannon get into an argument, Thomson falls, hits his head on the fireplace grate and dies. Fraser and Annie try to cover it up and make it look like an accident.

"Thomson and Martin Blecher have a disagreement about the course of the First World War at a local party and angry words are exchanged. Blecher by chance meets Thomson the next day on the Drummer Lake Portage. They have words again, and Blecher hits Thomson with a paddle and he dies."

Deemeester also adds, "According to current Ontario Parks government policy, all residential leaseholders will be obligated to either tear down or burn their buildings and ensure that the land is returned to its original state by 2017 — ironically 100 years after the death of Thomson."

There are many unexplained events on Canoe Lake. One young girl, Sarah, found a painting tucked in a crack in a tree and an old piece of wood inscribed with biblical quote. Does she have a Tom Thomson original? Who is creating mystical art in Algonquin Park?

There are power boats on the lake now. There are mysteries and there are many unanswered questions for curious visitors.

The Severn River Inn

~ Severn Bridge ~

LET ME TAKE YOU TO A TIME AND A PLACE OF MYSTERY, HISTORY, solitude, and peace. This is not necessarily linear time; perhaps it is eternal.

Welcome to the Severn River Inn at Severn Bridge, on the picturesque Severn River. May you enjoy an interesting holiday!

First — the river: the Severn River winds for 53 kilometres from Lake Simcoe through Lake Couchiching to Georgian Bay. Its namesake is a similar river winding through southwestern England. The First Nations called it Mujeduck.

The river came to be after the Wisconsin glacier and it was shallow in spots and more turbulent than it is today. The last century marked the growth of the Severn River into a gigantic waterway when a system was needed to make navigation possible from Lake Ontario to Georgian Bay. By the middle of the 19th century the river was also harnessed for power.

The Severn River Inn is a welcoming sight to contemporary visitors, as it overlooks the Severn River.

The first recorded pioneers came here in 1858. They were James H. Jackson, William Johnston, and John Young. They had all been given land grants on the river. By 1862 Severn Bridge was reported to be a thriving village site.

It was James H. Jackson who settled on the site where the Severn River Inn stands today. There he built a log cabin close to the river and opened a general store.

In January 1861 the Jackson store became Muskoka's very first post office and J.H. was the Postmaster. Three years later Jackson had fulfilled the requirements for his land grant and received a patent for all 95 acres of the combined lots 1 and 2 on the east side of the Muskoka Road.

With a mortgage of $500 from William Anderson, Jackson constructed a large, white, frame building which included his residence, the store and the post office.

The Northern Extension Railway arrived in 1873–74. It brought with it a new industry — tourism. Next came the steamboat *Pioneer*, making daily runs from Severn Bridge to campsites and hotels on Sparrow Lake and not far behind came other steamboats to accommodate the growing trade.

By 1896, Severn Bridge boasted a population of 150 people. More stores and shops opened to service the area residents, tourists, and the workers from mills that had been established on the river.

James Jackson passed away in 1894, and his son James H. Jackson Jr. took over the daily operations, which now included the telephone exchange. James Jr. knew that tourism would always be a good source of revenue and so he built a summer hotel to accommodate 35 to 40 guests. He named his hotel, which was situated on the bank of the river next to his residence, Riverview.

A disastrous fire in 1906, caused by a spark from the burner at the mill, levelled most of the village. The Jackson residence, store, post office, and hotel, along with many other homes and businesses were destroyed in a matter of minutes.

The merchants and villagers rallied to the task of rebuilding. By 1907, with the help of his brother, Joseph, who was a carpenter, James rebuilt a new brick building by the river, a building large enough once again to accommodate a store, a hotel, and a family residence. The establishment was named the Severn River Inn. This is now the third time for a building on one site.

It continued to be operated as a general store, a post office, and a telephone exchange, and they now boarded teachers, travellers, and summer guests. They were well known for their "Jackson hospitality." The inn became a thriving centre of social activity for the area.

James Jackson Jr. died in 1942 and the business was sold to his son-in-law, Arthur Fawcett, who had married James's daughter, Marjorie Jackson. Their daughter Pauline Delamere recalls growing up at the inn. "The teachers and guests ate their meals in the dining room, while the family dined in the kitchen. We had five rooms for lodgers to rent. They all shared one washroom, but there were two outhouses to use — one on one side of the building for men and another on the other side for the women to use. My grandmother Ida lived with us and resided on the second floor on the right-hand side of the front section of the building. She passed away in the inn ... but ... I don't recall any hauntings while my family lived there."

In 1972 the Fawcetts retired from business and sold the Severn River Inn. This was the first time in 110 years that it was out of the Jackson family. Since that time it has changed hands several times. Patricia Raymond purchased the place in 1981 and, with the help of her three children, she restored the building and opened a 10-room country inn.

Shortly thereafter, the Town of Gravenhurst declared the inn a Heritage Building under the Ontario Heritage Act. The original architectural features of the building have survived the passing of nine decades. The twin wooden posts, which supported the beam over the Victorian storefront of the general store, the original double-hung windows, the brick veneer, and the decorative columns on the long, screened verandah, now a summer dining area, still remain.

Eventually, Norman and Rosalie Rondeau and Curt and Kaaren Brandt purchased the historic inn. Both couples acknowledged that some unexplained activity certainly had been occurring in the building. However, no one, at that point, had sighted a ghost nor identified the spirits in question. Nevertheless, there were stories to verify a presence there.

Phyllis, an employee of the inn, had also worked for the previous owners. She had experienced mysterious happenings at the fire door. "I sometimes find the fire escape door, located at the front of the building, wide open. The door might open at night after the guests have retired and the patrons are gone. I have never seen a ghost, but I don't disbelieve — anything is possible."

Rosalie stated, "I get tapped on the shoulder in the back dining room area. This happens about once every two months." Her partner Kaaren, has heard children playing by the backstairs in the building but nothing was ever visible. There were no children physically present. "I could hear them running around and playfully squealing," she added. It was almost as if parallel lives were being lived or simultaneous activity was occurring, somewhat oblivious to the present day.

Kaaren has also experienced spirit activity on the grounds of the inn. "When I was raking leaves once, I felt someone tugging at my coat. I turned and said, 'If you'll be nice to me, I'll be nice to you!'"

Guests and patrons visiting the inn have the opportunity to explore several different settings in the building. They can enjoy a meal in the J.H. Jackson Dining Room, which was the original post office, the telephone exchange, and the general store, or they can just relax in the more formal parlour with a restful view of Severn River. The cozy Storefront lounge provides a turn-of-the-century atmosphere. The seven guest rooms, all beautifully furnished with antiques, are located on the second floor. One could almost step back in time themselves as the scene has been well set to do so. Could this be a key to keeping the past alive?

Gabriella Kira was the chef there in 1997 and she took great pride in her menu — prime rib on Sunday nights, the immensely popular beef Wellington, or the maritime seafood chowder prepared by her husband. Gabriella, herself, has had a number of experiences with spirit activity.

"One evening I was working with Rhonda. It was about eight o'clock and we were the only two people in the inn. We were in the bar area when we heard footsteps upstairs. Then we heard someone walking up and down the stairs by the back dining room, the stairs that lead to the second floor. The floors creak, so we know when someone is walking around. I also heard a door slam. It sounded like the door to either room 3 or 4. Rhonda said to me, 'Do you want to go upstairs to see who it is?' I said 'No!'"

"I think this spirit activity is so intriguing. Somehow it renders the previous inhabitants mysterious," Gabriella added.

One night Gabriella was working with Norman Rondeau. At the end of each day Norman would retire to the office on the second floor to complete the day's bookkeeping. At this time of the evening the business would be closed. On that particular night Norman and Gabriella were the only two people in the building.

Gabriella explained what happened, "I was downstairs in the basement taking some food out of the freezer for the next day. Suddenly I heard someone walking around in the bar area. I came upstairs, thinking it was Norman and then I realized he was still in the office. I asked Norman, if he had been downstairs, but the answer was no. I returned to the basement and again I heard the footsteps."

Gabriella took me to the basement, to show me how you can hear the footsteps of customers walking on the first floor. The sound of footsteps was quite pronounced.

As for Norman, although he had never seen a spirit appear, he had often heard mumbled voices. On another occasion, Norman, his mother Carol, and her sister Lillian were in the sitting room on the second floor when the lights went on and then off all by themselves.

Objects frequently went missing in the inn. Pictures hanging on the walls completely disappear. A special knife, used in the kitchen, disappeared and was never found. Gabriella's piping bag used for cake decorating also vanished never to be found. Who else had uses for these things and who changed the surroundings? Was there another setting, just beyond their view?

One evening at closing time, Rhonda went upstairs to check the rooms on the second floor. Walking along in the dark corridor she fell over a table in the middle of the hall. Someone had moved this piece of furniture away from the wall.

Norman's mother, Carol, and her husband often helped out around the inn. One day she was cleaning room 5. This room was well lit by natural sunlight during the day. Carol left the room and returned momentarily to discover that the lamp had been turned on. On another occasion she had been working and sat down in room 5 for a short rest. "I closed my eyes and the lights just came on by themselves," she explained.

It would seem that the inn is indeed a mysterious place of unexplained activity. Some people speculate that it is Pauline Delamere's grandmother, Ida, who died in the building. Other people have chosen to ignore the activity. If Pauline is right that there was no spiritual activity in the building before the 1970s, what could have caused it to start later?

When I returned in 2007, ten years after the writing of *Haunted Ontario*, I discovered that there had been many more experiences.

In August 2002 Pam Sulesky and her friend Sue MacLeod Browning arrived at the Severn River Inn. In the evening they had dinner on the back porch overlooking the picturesque Severn River. During their meal Pam's friend Sue saw something.

Pam explained, "My friend Sue is a gifted native healer from the First Nations Reserve of Curve Lake. That night she saw a woman in a blue dress with red hair worn up in a bun. She was walking along a balcony situated in front of the second-storey windows overlooking the river. This balcony doesn't exist today. I couldn't see this, but I didn't doubt what Sue had seen. She often sees things that most of us cannot.

"We strolled around the building after dinner to gaze at this beautiful building that must have had a wonderful past. When we looked at the structure from across the road Sue commented 'Look at the roof area.

What do you see?' I noticed a purple aura around the building. It was really strange."

The women then moved to the side of the house and encountered something. Pam observed, "I heard children laughing and squealing behind me. I turned quickly. It was a little startling, but there was no one there. At the same time I was looking for children that didn't exist, Sue noticed a man with a handle-bar mustache and wearing armbands on his sleeves. Again I couldn't see anything.

"Then we entered the inn and sat in the bar section. When the waitress came Sue asked her if the place was haunted. She went crazy. She called into the kitchen area to the cook and said 'these ladies have seen the ghosts.' The cook handed us a copy of *Haunted Ontario*. We were stunned. The Severn River Inn was in the book. The woman that Sue had seen in the back of the building was the ghost named Ida.

"That night as we walked around the second floor where we were staying the energy was undeniable, especially to anyone who has worked with energy before.

"Every time we would mention the name Ida, the lights would flicker in the sitting area of the second floor. Eventually I sat on the couch to enjoy a cup of tea, but we called it a night when something knocked the tea cup from my hand. It literally flew from my hand to the chair beside me. The feeling was similar to that of a magnetic pull."

This was only the beginning of the activity that night. Pam continued, "Once we moved into the room to call it a night, things began to happen. While we tried to sleep, we could hear the wind outside our window. The wind was blowing so hard it sounded as if there were a tornado outside. When Sue opened the drapes, it was still and calm outside. Under the bed, it sounded like someone was shuffling cards. It was so bizarre. Again, trying to get to sleep, I noticed someone had turned on the light in the hallway, as the door didn't meet the floor tightly. I could see the light coming under, into our room. I thought to myself, 'well, maybe they leave that light on for other guests'. Around 11:30 p.m., I was awakened by the sound of cutlery being sorted. I heard drawers opening and closing and the distinct sound of forks and knives being put away. Sue was already awake; she was worried because she could smell smoke. I couldn't smell it and I tried to put her mind at ease, but she was insistent. She thought there was a fire and ran out into the hallway to check and see if there were smoke detectors. All was quiet and normal outside our room, so she came back perplexed. Finally, sleep must have come because we awoke in the morning, although not too well rested.

"We went downstairs to enjoy our continental breakfast and spoke to the woman serving us about our strange and busy night. I'll never forget the feeling that washed over me when she told us we had been alone in the building since 9:30 p.m. the previous night. How could that be? Who turned on the light? Who was sorting cutlery? When Sue told her how she thought the building was on fire, the woman explained to us that the original house had burned down a hundred years ago. They had pushed the remains of the burned building into the river, and rebuilt the house we were in today. She told us that divers had been in the water that weekend and had brought some things out. I wondered if that might explain the dream I had had about a woman who gave me a china bunny rabbit with a beautiful burgundy and gold pattern on it. As well, I wondered if this diving group had stirred up the spirits who were watching so closely over their beloved home.

"After our breakfast, Sue went back to our room first to shower, change, and pack up. When she was finished I went up to have a shower. It seemed that the water had a mind of its own. While I was in the shower, mentally reviewing all the activities of the night before, the water completely shut off. I got out of the shower and tried the sink tap … nothing, no water. The whole time I could feel a presence around me. It wasn't scary, but it was definitely there. I wrapped myself up, and went into the hall and hollered down to Sue and the waitress about my dilemma. Sue went out into the yard, where the owner of the inn was watering the grass! Clearly, nothing was wrong with the water flow. He went down to the basement, checked all the pipes and could not figure out why, just in our room, the water would not run. I went back into the room … stood in the bathroom and said out loud, 'Ida, we have to leave … clean or dirty we have to leave. I promise to come back and visit again. Please let me get washed.' No word of a lie, I moved over to the shower, turned the handle and out came the water.

"I kept my promise to Ida and have been back to the inn a couple of times for lunch and dinner."

Contemporary photo of dining room interior, Severn River Inn

Pam's friend Sue shared some of her own observations from their stay at the Severn River Inn.

"While dining on the patio at the inn I looked up to the top of the building and noticed rays of grey/purple trailing up into the sky ... then what caught my eye was a woman who walked through the wall ... she was wearing 1800s type of clothing. She glanced down among the diners and simply walked back through the wall. Pam was now going 'what? What are you seeing?' I couldn't hide my expression. I told her we had visitors."

In December 2005 Norman and Rosalie, Curt and Kaaren sold the Severn River Inn to James and Wendy Fairbairn. James and Wendy were ready to leave the city life behind and live in the country. It just so happened that James's sister lived in Severn Bridge. When the inn went on the real estate market, his sister suggested they buy it. The Fairbairn's put an offer in and it was accepted. Both James and Wendy had restaurant backgrounds.

Currently James and Wendy offer four rooms to rent. The inn has two dining rooms and a lounge/bar area. Their chef is European-trained. The dinner menu features two dinner specialties each evening. It has

James and Wendy Fairbairn at the Severn River Inn

become well-known for excellent soups. The unique setting of the inn by the river provides a lovely location for weddings. They cater to small (50), intimate wedding festivities and corporate conferences.

The owners are well aware of the history and the hauntings of the inn. In fact, they are now part of a new chapter in the continuing ghostly experiences of visitors and overnight guests.

Wendy shared an early encounter of unexplained activity that occurred in the spring of 2005. "We had just installed a French door near the entrance to the inn. It was a self closing door. Two weeks later, at closing time, James and I were sitting at the bar when we noticed that the new door was ajar. This shouldn't be happening!"

Wendy decided to go and check the door. As she stood up they both watched the door close on its own. Wendy explained, "The door does not stay open. It was as if someone was holding the door open."

Last September a woman who was driving by the inn, on Highway 11, felt compelled to turn off the road and visit the inn. James stated what happened next. "This woman came in and sat at the bar. She announced almost immediately that she could feel something there. She asked, 'tell me about the two women.'"

James was taken aback by the woman's request. James continued the account, "I told her about our chef who at the time resided in room 1. The chef had said that in the two years he had been there, he would occasionally hear two women arguing with each other outside his door. On each occasion he was the only person in the building."

The woman decided to stay for the evening. She asked James to tell her about the boat.

James added, "The only thing I could think of was the steamer that once travelled the river taking guests to Stanton House on Sparrow Lake."

The woman responded, "There was a man on that boat who was having an affair with a younger woman and that is why the women were arguing in the hallway."

Then she asked James if she could see the upstairs of the inn.

James recounted. "I took her upstairs and showed her around. She said she felt a very strong presence upstairs. The spirit, she thought, was transient. She commented, 'They don't live here.' She then walked down the hallway feeling the walls with her hands. She felt a strong presence coming from room 5. Then we went down to rooms 7 and 8. She stood in the hallway between the doors and commented, 'There is a very strong energy flow between these two rooms.'"

Wendy added, "These two rooms would have been the original living space of the Jackson family. This was where Ida lived."

James stated what happened next. "We entered room 7. The woman walked up to a wicker chair in the room and touched it. Then she spoke, 'The person sitting in this chair doesn't like me.' I just said 'okay.' We left the room and entered the little hallway that leads to room 5. She stood and faced room 5 and observed, 'Someone had an accident right here. I also see someone with a noose.'"

As far as James was concerned no one had ever died in the building in that manner. He had heard that someone had hanged themselves in the barn that once stood across the street.

Then she left the inn.

James mentioned an experience a former housekeeper had had while cleaning a room. "She wouldn't say what room. The guests had had a party in the room. The room was quite messy. The housekeeper had felt a heaviness or tension in the room. When she was standing by the doorway she was tapped on the shoulder. She looked around, but no one was there. Then she felt the heaviness leave the room."

A group of employees from Manual Life were once involved in a conference at the inn. One person in the group kept teasing another member of their group about ghosts.

James shared what happened next. "By late evening everyone went off to bed. The man who had tormented his friend about ghosts earlier in the evening was the first to appear in the morning. He looked like he had never slept. During the night his cell phone would ring and it lit up on several occasions, but then it would shut off. He was staying in room 5. He heard noises during the night and felt extremely uncomfortable. He refused to stay there any longer and left the conference." And the stories continue ....

Was it disturbing for the spirits to have a rapid succession of owners? Did that stir them up? Or was it divers? Activity in these places I have visited is definitely still occurring and would actually seem to be on the increase. Is this because of the time in which we live or has writing about ghosts actually stirred them up and made them more powerful? Does the opportunity to be acknowledged appeal to those who need somehow to communicate? Thoughts to ponder — a little history and a little mystery exist here, so stop and see which era it might be that you will visit.* You might find a new mystery of your own.

The Severn River Inn is currently closed.

The Mackenzie Inn

~ Kirkfield ~

Author's note: A name in this chapter has been changed to respect the privacy of a "sensitive" who felt presences in the house. Another individual is not named at all in order to protect the identity of a man who may have been falsely accused, here, of a horrible crime.

IT MUST HAVE SEEMED LIKE A DREAM TO THE VILLAGERS OF KIRKFIELD, Ontario, when in 1888, William Mackenzie built a forty-room mansion in their midst. To this day one can marvel at the sight.

This mansion still holds a spell over this tiny settlement in Victoria County. There is a power there, a veil of intrigue and mystery that permeates the house and grounds. One can sense "something" when one crosses the threshold, a feeling, a premonition of the unveiled.

The Mackenzie Inn, as it is referred to today, reflects an era now gone, an era when money could buy whatever you desired. And it is a fact that those who created this grandeur have not left it. The surrounding area is also steeped in Scottish lore and so, whatever you do, never let anyone step on your shadow!

My first acquaintance with the Mackenzie mansion occurred when I was researching a book on old Ontario homesteads in 1979. I remember how this building caught my eye and how I was drawn to stop and inquire. As majestic as it was, its one-time presence was also obviously faded; I was hooked.

A warm Irish family, the MacDonald-Rosses, owned the estate at that time, including the gatehouse, which had been turned into a restaurant, and the log cabin across the street. They worked day and night to save the estate from ruin. Their earnest efforts were, eventually, fruitless and they, too, had their misfortunes and left. The MacDonald-Rosses had become part of the failed dream, part of the mystery and intrigue. To those who dream, this mansion is a castle.

Sir William Mackenzie, Canada's railway baron, dreamed the first dream. The story began with John Mackenzie, born in 1810, in Ross-shire, Scotland. In 1832, John and his wife left Scotland for Canada where they landed first in Montreal, and then Toronto. In late 1836 they were assigned two lots in Eldon Township, Victoria County, and the family settled there.

According to parish records, William Mackenzie was born in a log cabin on October 17, 1849, although he later claimed his date of birth to be October 30. His mother, Mary, died when he was three and William went to live with his mother's sister, Catherine. He completed his education at grammar school in Lindsay.

In 1868 he taught for a year in Bolsover and then moved to Kirkfield. At the age of 21 he began a new career with his brother Alex and his classmates, John and Angus McDonald. They opened the Shoofly Store, so-called because William was constantly shooing flies away. This young group of men supplied timber for bridges and for wooden roads, as the northern part of Victoria County and the district of Muskoka became populated.

In the 1870s William and his brothers operated a sawmill, a sash and door factory, a grist mill, and a small furniture company in Kirkfield. Their entire operation covered all parts of the industry from raw materials to finished product. They also had an exclusive license to cut timber in areas prohibited to others — no competitors!

The Mackenzie Inn as it appears today.

In 1872 William married a woman of rare beauty and quiet dignity; she was a local Catholic girl, Margaret Merry. They had a private ceremony in Lindsay without benefit of family; two strangers witnessed their vows. He was a Presbyterian and their families did not approve of the union. The Mackenzies had a long and happy marriage and raised nine children.

Between 1874 and 1876 William and Alex Mackenzie constructed bridges for the Victoria Railway, as well as the station and engine house in Kinmount, north of Lindsay. They were beginning to prosper financially.

William Mackenzie set out for Winnipeg in 1882 to set up a branch of the Mackenzie Brothers. Two years later he met his future partner, Donald Mann. These were railroad boom times. One of Mackenzie's major projects was the construction of the Mountain Creek Bridge, one of the largest wooden structures ever built over a gorge in Western Canada.

After 1886 he and his associates were granted major construction contracts on numerous railways and by 1895 he was one of Canada's leading railway barons and financiers.

His rise in economic stature helped to inspire his dream home. In 1888 William Mackenzie started construction of the splendid three-storey mansion that graces the main street of Kirkfield today. This was an extravagant structure measuring 1,400 square metres (13,000 square feet) with 40 rooms, two bathrooms and nine fireplaces. The cost was $18,000. Upon entering this home, one found oneself in a large reception area and from there one could be escorted to the parlour for tea and conversation, the dining room for a meal, or perhaps to the kitchen. An oak staircase found its way to the second floor and servants were housed on the third floor.

Some folks say that a tunnel under the building led underground across the street to the home of Margaret's sister, Mrs. Mitchell. At any rate, Margaret Mackenzie was in her glory. She had come from a poor family in the district and now found herself with 13 servants to attend to her needs and whims. Money and fame, the townsfolk speculated, had gone to her head. People could see that she had become very ambitious. In 1993 Jennie Harrigan Manen, at the age of 97, recalled Margaret Mackenzie in her own memoirs, "She bought most of the farms adjoining Kirkfield. Each farm had a man working it. This was all on a grand scale, wages were good, the house free, there was a dairy farm and a racing stable. A golf course was set out on the sandy hills across from the cemetery. The two hotels were torn down and a large edifice called the Kirkfield Inn was built. Of course, the locals were not exactly welcome there, nor would they feel at home in such elegant surroundings."

In 1912 Margaret Mackenzie had, indeed, torn down the two original hotels in town and perhaps one of the reasons the locals didn't feel welcome was because she had imposed a ban on alcohol being served in any public building in the village of Kirkfield. Her Kirkfield Inn, of course, did not sell alcohol. One can imagine the resentment felt by some residents. The locals were forced, for "refreshment," to ride to Bolsover to visit a female bootlegger by the name of Biddy Young. Ms. Young was not too fond of the Mackenzies and was heard to say on the village streets of Kirkfield that the Mackenzies had forgotten their humble beginnings. She felt she was blessed with second sight and she "saw" that one day the Mackenzie family would experience doom and gloom. Unfortunately for William and Margaret, time has proven her to be right.

Nevertheless, the Mackenzie's fortunes flourished and they continued to live luxuriously. They purchased property on Balsam Lake, built a massive summer home and docked a yacht on the lake. Their impressive mansion in Toronto was called Benvenuto. Rumours about other investments abounded and the villagers, perhaps envious of their prosperity, felt that some investments might be unsavoury. None of this has been substantiated, however.

The locals in Kirkfield continued to feel the effects of Margaret's strong influence. She not only imported trees and flowers from all over the world for her house, but also planted 600 maple trees along the streets of Kirkfield. To insure that these saplings did not fall prey to "inconsiderations," she had the town officials impose a twenty-dollar fine for anyone caught tying a horse to a maple tree. She was sensitive in the extreme about the appearance of Kirkfield, and, so it seemed to the residents, oblivious to the feelings of others. If a home did not meet her standards for respectability, it was not unusual for a crew of men to arrive one day to paint the house at her request and expense, without the homeowner's permission!

In 1895 William and Donald Mann organized and built the Canadian Northern Railway, which later became a transcontinental system. At that time he was said to be the second-richest man in all of Canada.

William continued to build his empire. He was a partner in the Toronto Street Railway and an early investor with Sir Henry Pellatt (famous for Casa Loma in Toronto) in hydro-electric power. He owned a fleet of ocean-going ships and was the founder of a Brazilian power and light company that eventually emerged as Brascan and he was its first chairperson.

William Mackenzie and Donald Mann were knighted by King George V in 1911.

In 1914 Sir William and family were in England. It was Tuesday, August 4, 1914, when they heard the news that the German army had crossed into Belgium. Britain and her empire were now at war. William was heard to say "I'm finished." In a short time his transcontinental railway empire and other business enterprises faced serious financial crisis as a result of world events.

Sir William saw his empire crumble during World War I. And on June 14, 1917, Prime Minister Borden informed him that his railway would have to be nationalized. The government could no longer financially assist his railway dreams. He was, on all accounts, exhausted, and Lady Mackenzie was gravely ill with cancer. She had just undergone surgery and he had kept a ten-day vigil at her bedside. When he heard the news from the Prime Minister he lowered his head and wept.

The Mackenzie family, date unknown.

On November 29, 1917, Lady Mackenzie died at Benvenuto. Her body was taken by train to Gamebridge, where two horses and a light wagon took her body on to a burial place in the Kirkfield Cemetery.

Sir William Mackenzie died five years later on December 5, 1923. He, too, was taken by train and horse and wagon to be buried beside his beloved wife.

It took years for the estate to be settled. Eventually, Sir William's heirs inherited about $800,000 — a far cry from the value of his estate in the 1890s.

In less than a decade after his death, Benvenuto was demolished. In January 1925 a whole business block of Kirkfield was burned to the ground. The next month the Kirkfield Inn was gutted by fire.

Joe Mackenzie, Sir William's son, sold the Kirkfield home in 1927 for one dollar to the Sisters of St. Joseph. He was killed a very short time later in a car accident just outside Kirkfield. The estate remained a convent/orphanage until the 1970s when it was purchased by the MacDonald-Ross family.

In 1936, the historic village hall was burned to the ground. The *Wawinette*, Sir William's impressive yacht on Balsam Lake was sold to a hockey hero in the 1930s. He and his friends were boating on southern Georgian Bay when they hit a rock, the boat sank, and 20 lives were lost.

The golf course disappeared under vegetation and the dairy barn was vandalized. The racing stable was eventually demolished. By the 1960s the Mackenzie's summer home on Balsam Lake had gone to rack and ruin.

Biddy Young probably had no idea how true her prophecy would ring.

The Kirkfield estate itself has known several different owners at different times. By the time Paul and Joan Scott discovered it, the estate was in a sad condition. The Scotts knew they were destined to own it, however. They, too, had been drawn into the mists of time and had envisioned the estate in its grandeur. As if by magic they could see it! They could also see what few can sense — a presence! They restored the home, furnished it with antiques, and opened a bed and breakfast.

The Scotts had a passion for preserving old buildings and history. Paul loved to tell a story and was quite at home on the Mackenzie estate. If the interest was there, Paul toured his guests and other tourists through the old building, sharing the Mackenzie story. Sometimes others had stories too — ghost stories!

I had often reminisced by the fire in the front room of the old house with the MacDonald-Ross family, as they recounted stories of bumps in the night and eerie noises in the gatehouse. The stories always seem to match the atmosphere. Is Sir William still here or is it Lady Mackenzie who walks the halls of the manor? Are they unable to leave their dream?

The Scotts had been open just over a year when a young woman we will call "Julia" registered for bed and breakfast at the inn. While she sat on the front veranda the next day Julia asked Paul, "Is this house haunted?"

Taken aback for a moment, Paul hesitantly responded with "I'm not sure." He then asked her what she did for a living.

Julia answered, "I am a musician of sorts, an ordained minister, a writer, and a house cleaner."

She explained that she wasn't a house cleaner in the traditional sense. Julia could feel the presence of spirits in a house and, if necessary, clean them out. She is what is sometimes called a "sensitive". Julia could feel the presence of spirits in this particular house and asked Paul if he would explore the premises with her.

How could he refuse? On their tour her feelings were strongest around the long-unused third floor. When the Scotts first bought the place, plaster was missing from some of the walls and there were gaps in the floor boards. Originally the third floor had housed the Mackenzie servants and a nursery and it was also used later by the nuns. This section of the home was eventually restored by Paul and Joan to house some of their overnight guests and the area included five bedrooms, a bathroom, and a large sitting room space. Each room was named for places and characters associated with the Mackenzies and their business accomplishments.

Once on the third floor, Julia exclaimed, "Oh, I don't like the individual who lived in that bedroom (now called The Tony Griffin Room) to the right. He was a cruel and very sick person. And he is still here in his room."

They then turned left and climbed three steps into the main section of the third floor. Julia looked into the bathroom on the right and turned to peek into the bedroom across the way. Immediately she remarked, "I hear children laughing and babies crying. This must have been the nursery." She was right!

An old rocking chair sat in that room and Julia could see a little old lady sitting there. She said the woman had shocking white hair. Paul explained that this rocking chair had belonged to his Aunt Miriam. After she died he had been given that chair. Julia clearly described his Aunt Miriam. He added, "On two separate occasions last year, customers saw a little old lady sitting in this platform rocker with bright white hair." Had Aunt Miriam stayed with her chair?

Julia and Paul proceeded to a small room on the left. She said this room had once been used to store trunks. Straight ahead was a room (The Canadian Northern Room) overlooking the main street. Julia felt this to be a very peaceful room.

The sitting room was located in the middle of the third floor. Another room off the sitting room also overlooked the main street. This room was called the George Laidlaw Room. Julia sensed it to be the "most serene room in the house." Paul added, "We have people who come into this room and automatically feel entranced."

A rocking chair belonging to a deceased aunt of the current owners sits in one of the guest rooms at the Mackenzie Inn. Several guests have reported seeing the chair rocking on its own, seemingly powered by an unseen force.

The next bedroom was the TTC Room. Julia felt this room to be a very uncomfortable space and although she sensed something there she was unable to describe her feelings.

Directly across from the Laidlaw Room was a small storage room that still housed the old water system of the house. Outside this doorway Julia began to quiver and weep. She could not move, she was traumatized. "I won't go in there. Someone has been abused and murdered here. She was drowned."

Paul was caught by surprise and didn't know what to say. Meanwhile, Julia was feeling enormous pressure on her head, her knees felt weak, there were shivers up the back of her neck; she could not enter the room!

"She started to tremble. Tears welled up in her eyes," stated Paul. "I can't, I can't go in there — there is too much trauma. It's overwhelming me with sadness. I see a little girl choking, no, drowning. Yes, drowning, death, sadness, Oh, I can't stay up here any longer," Julia uttered.

Paul asked Julia what he could do about this newfound presence in the house. She replied, "You could try taking out all the wood in the room as it has absorbed the negative vibrations or another way might be to put out containers of Epson Salts. They might absorb the negative vibes."

Paul added, "Tearing out all the wood wasn't really an option so we proceeded to buy a large quantity of Epson Salts. This often prompted questions from people who toured this area in the year that we tried this solution, but as the many unsolicited stories of feelings and sensations kept coming from those who had no knowledge of the situation we summarized that it wasn't working. The salts were removed."

Paul showed me this storage room. Just inside is a place for cleaning supplies. To the left of this space is a small doorway that leads to a room containing the old water system — a 2,000-gallon, lead-lined water cistern! The entire space felt odd, especially since I already knew Julia's story. Julia felt that the trauma felt by the victim had been impregnated into the very fibre of the room.

Paul elaborated, "The next year a friend of mine came up for a visit from Florida. One day he ventured into this space that Julia refused to enter and he remarked to me, 'Paul, do you know a six-year-old was drowned in this cistern?'

"I asked him, 'How would you know this?'

"He replied, 'It simply came to me while I was in there. And furthermore, the individual responsible was demented.'"

Paul returned to the story about Julia, "The next day Julia and I were on the veranda. She looked me straight in the eye and wanted to know if I was related to a man she named. She said he was the man who lived on the third floor. I told her I was not but I would ask around."

Paul discovered that there was once a man by that name who worked on the estate at one time. He lived in the back room on the third floor. There was no logical reason for Julia to have come up with his name.

There is no evidence of a young girl either missing or later found murdered in Kirkfield. If this did indeed occur, it was more than a well-kept secret. If Julia and Paul's friend from Florida are correct, however, there was a murderer who lived freely among the residents of Kirkfield.

The Gatehouse Restaurant was located on one side of the property. The structure has been used as a school as well as a restaurant. This building was reputed to be haunted by spirits as long ago as the 1970s. Back then people said they heard noises in the back kitchen on the ground floor and footsteps on the second floor.

Leigh Hazelton was an employee of the restaurant and shared some haunting information with me, "I see a little girl appear under the counter on the first floor of the restaurant. She has short hair and very dirty legs. She would be about six or seven years old. One would think she was real, until she disappears."

Could this be the little girl from the main house?

"I hear noises all the time, like banging. This always occurs downstairs at 10:00 a.m. I have also heard someone walking around upstairs, the radio goes off by itself downstairs, upstairs the radio changes stations on its own and the hot water tap in the ladies' washroom goes on by itself.

"When we were renovating the upstairs of the building we had the oddest thing happen. We had just hung a number of decorative plates on the wall. As we turned to leave, one plate flew across the room. This was impossible — we had them securely hooked."

Paul talked about other unexplained activity in the main building. The Scotts had had some difficulty with the electrical panel on the second floor. Paul described what happened, "On two occasions all the breakers switched off on the panel. I called in an electrician to show him what had happened. He told me it was impossible for all the breakers to go off at once.

"Shortly afterward this same electrical panel switched off again. At this point I recalled a woman on a bus tour telling me about the ghost in her house. One day the spirit dropped an antique clock on the floor. She was furious and shouted at it. Since that time she has not had any breakage. I decided to do the same thing. I went into a shouting rage and since that time the breakers have never switched off."

The Sir William Room, located on the second floor, is another area of activity. A female guest heard the flapping of slippers going down the hall near the doorway; other guests have felt a male presence in the room. Some people believed Sir William, who once occupied this room, was still there.

Terry Burton lives in the village of Kirkfield and was employed in 1995 by the Scott family to assist in numerous duties. I interviewed her and she had this to say. "Last summer I was working on the third floor dusting and cleaning the TTC Room. Suddenly the door slammed shut. I panicked and told the ghost that I was a friend and to leave me alone. One time when I was vacuuming on the third floor in the sitting room, I felt the pressure of someone trying to push me off balance. I turned around, but nothing was there. Every so often I sense a vibration, like someone is there with me. One time I went to clean one of the rooms on the third floor and it was locked. There are no keys to the rooms on this floor, they all lock from the inside."

I asked Terry how she felt about the storage and cistern room. She replied, "I don't like that room. The door is always opening on its own!"

In October 1999 Paul and Joan were involved in a séance at the inn.

A warm, inviting fire burned in the living room fireplace. The candles were lit and the lights were dimmed. A medium by the name of Sandra proceeded to go into a deep, sleep-like trance. The following proceedings were recorded in Paul Scott's book entitled *A Decade of Memories*.

Sandra's friend Ernie began the session by stating "Hello, and who do we have with us? What is your name? We are here to help you."

The presence of a spirit was soon felt. Ernie asked, "And who do we have with us? What is your name? This is Joyce, Rick, Joan, and Paul. I am Ernie. We are your friends and are here to try and help you."

Again he asked, "What is your name and how did you come to us?"

Then a little girl spoke. "I saw you arrive tonight. I was in the front room window upstairs and you went to the wrong gate. It was closed." She giggled impishly.

Ernie replied, "Yes you are right. We missed the open gate and went to the restaurant gate. Now tell us, who are you and what is your name?"

The girl stated, "I, I don't remember my name. But Nellie calls me 'Sweetie.' You can call me Sweetie."

Ernie asked, "Who is Nellie?"

"Oh, she is my friend. She is upstairs. She is happy, she likes to knit. She knits all the time. Nellie and I are friends," added the girl.

Ernie inquired, "Do you have any other friends?"

She replied, "No, Nellie is my only friend. She never leaves her chair in her room, but I do."

Ernie asked, "Would you like to see your friends again and perhaps your mother and father?"

She stated, "Oh yes, but I don't remember my mother and father and I haven't seen my friends for a long time. I think I would like an apple, apples are my favourite and I haven't had an apple for a long time."

Ernie asked her to look around and tell the group what she could see.

"I see a pretty lady. She is smiling and she is pointing to a bright light."

Ernie told the girl to go with the pretty lady and see all of her friends.

Paul then added, "Sandra (the medium) was relaxed again as if waiting for her next challenge. It came quickly. Sandra took on an entirely different air. She was haughty and abrupt. She was definitely upset about being in our lowly presence but also curious as to who we were and what we were doing in Mother Superior's office."

Ernie asked, "And who are you? What is your name?"

The spirit replied, "And who might you be?"

Ernie introduced the group again.

"My name is Sister Florence, if you must know. I am here doing God's work. I am in charge here."

Ernie acknowledged Sister Florence and asked, "How many are you in charge of?"

Sister Florence disclosed, "There were 27 here at roll call this morning, but one has left. Now we have 26."

Ernie said, "Do you realize, Sister, that you are dead? You are in the spirit world. Would you like to go and be with your friends and family?"

Sister Florence stated, "What are you saying? I would know if I was dead. I am needed here to do God's work."

Paul added, "As she was saying this Sandra's head went down and then back up as Sister Florence continued."

"What has happened? Why am I dressed in these clothes? This is most unusual," added the Sister.

Again Ernie told the Sister she was dead.

Sister Florence then added, "No, no — I can't be — who would replace me here if I went. No, I am needed here."

Ernie added, "Is there no one you could leave in your place, maybe for a short time? If you don't like it, you could return. Look around. What do you see?"

Sister Florence answered, "Why, I see a beautiful baby and she is pointing to a bright light. She has such a pretty smile. Perhaps I could ask Sister Margaret to tend my duties. She might be able to look after things here for a short time. Give me a moment, I will ask her."

A short time passes. Sister Florence returns speaking through Sandra. Sister Margaret would take over until she returned.

According to Paul, "Sandra then seemed to relax again and then she came to life with a vengeance. Her voice was much deeper and her language was quite obscene. Sandra sat up even more boldly than ever before. She was defiant and coarse."

Ernie than asked, "Who are you? What is your name?"

The spirit interjected, "I know who you are. I won't tell you my name. I will tell you this. I am really glad that bitch is gone. She was always telling me what to do. Perhaps I can have some peace now. Do this — do that — I don't know why I am back."

Ernie asked, "Oh, where were you?"

The spirit replied, "I worked here as a custodian, but I got tired of it and went to the East coast. I don't know why I came back — work, work, work, never an idle moment."

Ernie wondered if this unhappy soul would like to leave.

The spirit wasn't interested. "No God damned way; you're not sending me anywhere."

Paul then added, "Sandra went limp. The spirit was gone. But the question on everyone's mind was where did he go!"

The other question on everyone's mind was did a Sister Florence ever exist? Had she actually worked here at the old Mackenzie estate?

In the past Joan and Paul had met previous students of the convent and some Sisters, but never a mention of Sister Florence. A coffee table book entitled *As the Tree Grows* was presented to Paul and Joan by the Sisters of Peterborough. The book highlighted the accounts of all the convents they had operated.

Paul added, "We had both had a quick read of the very interesting story about Kirkfield, St. Margaret's section, but didn't remember any mention of a Sister Florence. We read the story again with much more attention to names. There it was, 'Sister Florence,' an obscure mention that she was the first Sister to come to St. Margaret's. Strangely enough, the last Sister to work here was Sister Margaret."

This event was followed-up by more coincidences. Paul and Joan were visited by a man named Frank and his wife from Oshawa. Frank had seen the name Mackenzie on their van. He knew of the Mackenzie estate as well as knowing the Mackenzie family. During an afternoon they exchanged stories. Just as they were about to leave Frank asked, "Whatever happened to Nellie?"

Paul added, "We were shocked to hear this name so soon after our paranormal experience which sent dear Sweetie off to a better place. Sweetie was so fond of Nellie. Nellie was still with us in the St. Margaret Room on the third floor, sitting in my Aunt Miriam's platform rocker and at peace doing her knitting."

Frank explained that Nellie was a servant that worked for the Mackenzie's, one whom they had met during a visit to the Mackenzie's cottage on Balsam Lake.

So who else has seen Nellie?

According to Paul, "We have had a number of reports from the St. Margaret Room of unusual happenings. One young woman announced at breakfast, somewhat matter-of-factly, she was awakened at about 1:00 p.m. to find herself in a wash of bright light. The room was the same only the furniture was different. The dresser was covered with children's toys and she felt a sense of peace and joy.

"Two woman guests, on different occasions, reported being awakened by the sounds of excited conversation just outside their door, young people laughing."

Paul described the experience of one employee who had worked at the inn for the past seven years, but wouldn't clean the rooms on the third floor if she was alone in the house.

The Gatehouse as it appears today.

"She has been physically bounced around and one time was locked out of a room that was empty. She has frequently seen a big old grey cat in the kitchen area."

Joan, on one occasion, saw an apparition. Paul added, "It was a fleeting glance of a man in a safari-style outfit."

The spiritual activity on the estate does not end there. Many people have reported seeing a nun walking the grounds. They see her walking from the house toward the gatehouse. According to their reports, she looks real. Obviously, one nun who lived and worked on the estate still remains behind. Unfortunately, we may never know why.

In June 2001 Sharon Arnaud and Jeremy Pierpoint arrived at the Mackenzie Inn with the intent of leasing the Gatehouse Restaurant and eventually purchasing the entire estate. Paul added, "Both Jeremy and Sharon were psychologists and were planning to be married on July 1, 2001. Their plans were to have a garden wedding at their home in Argyle. Once Sharon saw our grounds and especially Apostles Row, she was hooked on having her wedding at the inn.

"Sharon and Jeremy moved quickly to begin renovations of the restaurant. The whole building was scheduled for a face-lift. Lights were burning many nights after we turned in and sometimes they worked clear through to 6:00 a.m. and then carried on a regular workday. These people impressed us with their hard work ethics and their great ideas," stated Paul.

Negotiations were ongoing between Paul, Joan, Sharon, and Jeremy over the purchase of the entire estate. In the fall of 2001, Paul and Joan handed the keys over to Sharon and Jeremy.

In January 2007 I returned to the Mackenzie Inn to interview Jeremy about any recent hauntings.

Jeremy described the vision he and Sharon had for the Mackenzie Inn. "It was to make the place a premiere wedding destination."

Jeremy certainly acknowledges the presence of spirits in the inn and on the grounds. He believes, "The spiritual energy here is quite welcoming."

He feels their changes to the décor of the gatehouse might have stirred up some energy at the time. He added, "One night I was in the little office on the second floor of the Gatehouse Restaurant. I heard the downstairs door open and close. I yelled down, 'Sharon I'm up here.' No answer. I went downstairs and was overcome by a feeling of someone else right there in my space.

"That same week I came downstairs and then heard footsteps upstairs. When I went to investigate no one was there."

In the main estate building, the staff, including Jeremy, commented about how uncomfortable they feel in the basement room where the furnace is located.

In 2003 Jeremy actually encountered an entity in the inn. "I was getting something out of the storage room. I was coming back through into the kitchen and this voice stated, 'Are you okay?' That was it.

"The next week I was coming into the kitchen area again. I saw this grey swish or irregular shape — a fleeting misty apparition and then it was gone."

Just a couple of days later Jeremy was coming into the kitchen through the back door and there it was again — this misty shape by the doorway.

Jeremy continued, "That summer we had a local woman employed for the weddings. Her 16-year-old son also worked here. During one wedding the son was upstairs on the second floor. He was seated in the landing area and was reading a magazine. At about 9:00 p.m. a ten- or 11-year-old went by him and on upstairs. The young lad realized the kid is out of place. He was wearing earrings like a gypsy and outdated clothing. He realized the boy never really looked at him. Later he told his mother about it and she responded by telling him there were no children on site during the wedding festivities."

In fall 2006, a young couple who were celebrating their first wedding anniversary arrived at the Mackenzie Inn. Sharon and Jeremy booked them in the Lucy Maude Montgomery Room. This room was the infirmary during the convent years.

Jeremy described what happened next. "The couple decided to relax in their room for the evening. There were three tea lights in glass holders placed on the fireplace mantle. They lit them at about 8:00 p.m.

"The couple fell asleep at 12:30 a.m. They woke up at 1:30 a.m. to the smoke alarm ringing in their room. They glanced about and saw that the oil painting hanging over the mantelpiece was on fire. The tea lights were burning, but the candles had long burned out. The husband turned the light on. At that precise moment there was nothing wrong with the painting. There was no smoke in the air. The smoke detector had stopped ringing. The energy had cleared. Everything was back to normal."

In fall 2003, medium Bette Gray of the Labyrinth Resource Centre in Lindsay and her friend Kathryn of the *Lindsay Post* visited the Mackenzie Inn for the first time.

Bette has been "seeing" and doing readings from an early age. Her mother had the gift to see. At about age 13, Bette began to see and hear things that other people couldn't. It is quite startling what Bette encountered at the inn.

"When I entered the premises I knew I was going to do a reading for someone. There was a female spirit around. A woman who was associated with someone in the house. I went to the main floor bathroom. There were children around me in the hall. There was a closet across from the bathroom that was concealed by a curtain. I saw this young girl peeking out at me. She would have been about eight years old.

"Then we went back to meet Sharon and Jeremy in the library. I ended up doing a reading for Sharon. Afterward we went on a tour of the mansion.

"We went upstairs to Lady Mackenzie's Room. The same little girl I had seen earlier was following us. Then she went into the corner of the closet in the room. Next we visited the Count de Lesseps' Room to the left. I saw an old lady there. I believe she was a nun. She wouldn't communicate with me. She disappeared into the wall.

"Then we entered Sir Williams' Room. I sensed a vortex here. I received an electrical zap from my earring in my ear. Obviously, they didn't want to communicate.

"Next was the maids' room at the end of the hall. There is a wonderful healing energy in that room. I heard a voice say, Margaret or Maggie. This was a lady with the Mackenzie family — like a servant. She had some personal relationship with William. Perhaps she was the head maid. She told me we were in her room.

"Then we went upstairs to the third floor. I wanted to just play hide and seek. There were children all around me. Where I was standing with my hand on the doorway to where the water cistern is located, I heard a child speak. The child was telling me that they had been drowned. There was a big investigation. They tried to charge someone with murder, but later it was reduced to neglect. Suddenly a sister appeared and slammed the door out of my hands.

"Then we went down the back stairs to the kitchen. I went out to the front porch. There I encountered Sir William. He was telling me that the little house out front was originally a playhouse. He loved his family dearly. He had a good sense of humour. He was a man of his time. He had one daughter he favoured who was very polite and well-spoken.

"Then we went for tea. I could see candles burning everywhere in the room. I was told later that this was once the chapel."

Each year Bette organizes Psychic Development Meetings at the Mackenzie Inn. A group of participants spend a couple days at the inn sensing the spiritual energies of the estate. Bette highlighted some of the activity of the past two years.

On one occasion a very large orb was seen moving from the left to right and circling the second floor at about 11:00 p.m. Other orbs have been seen in the main hall and dining room. One of their younger male participants was visited by a very friendly female spirit during the night. It seemed that she really liked him.

During one of their investigations in the cellar, some of the attendees found the energy too dense and had to leave. A little later, they met the man who was part of the not-so-nice energy. He identified himself as a groundskeeper that had been employed there. He smelt of strong homemade alcohol.

One way or another, the Mackenzie Inn is very haunted. All sorts of stories continue to be written and told about the Mackenzies, about the estate, and about the village. After all these years their Mackenzie presence is still felt. The hauntings still continue despite the séances. It is not always a simple case of sending a spirit to the light. In fact, dimensional travel could very well account for the paranormal activity. Guests are simply encountering another dimension of time. What a location and what an opportunity!

The Prince George Hotel

~ Kingston ~

SINCE MANKIND FIRST BEGAN TO THINK AND WRITE ABOUT MORTALITY so many theories have developed about where the spirits or soul of a being goes after death. A popular and poetic idea, acceptable to the religious and agnostic alike, is that the mortal remains are sent back to their beginnings "ashes to ashes, dust to dust" while the spirit may linger for a time, even if it is only in the hearts of those it has left behind.

Not all spirits linger for a short time. The inability to let go of love may keep them walking the halls and passageways of their memories.

Such was the fate of Lily Herchemer of Kingston, a young girl entranced by the roving eyes of a sailor.

The Herchemer family were among the first settlers to own and operate a business on the waterfront. The port of Kingston in 1800 was a rather unlawful place. After all, Kingston had already seen its fair share of war and political change. Sailors drank to forget the long rough voyages and sought out the company of prostitutes to ease their loneliness.

Saloons and houses of ill-repute cropped up along the waterfront.

It hadn't always looked this way. The settlement was originally a fort and fur-trading post in the 1670s when Count Frontenac, governor of New France, oversaw the construction of Fort Frontenac. Sieur de la Salle was put in charge of the fort in 1674, and he set about building a settlement that housed 50 craftsmen and labourers next to the fort walls.

In 1758 Fort Frontenac was captured by the British under Colonel John Bradstreet. The entire settlement was abandoned for twenty-five years. Major John Rose arrived in 1783 to restore the fort to its former status. Surveyor John Collins followed closely behind and laid out the future town, a town soon to be settled by United Empire Loyalists.

The Native people who inhabited the area called this land Cataraqui, meaning "rocks standing in water." A deal was struck with the Mississauga First Nations for the purchase of the land along the lakeshore westward from Cataraqui. In exchange for this territory they were promised yearly payments of clothing, blankets, guns, and household articles.

The following Captain Michael Gross arrived with the first group of loyalist settlers — 95 men, 39 women, 78 children, and 8 servants. (In those days, servants were obviously considered genderless.) The settlement grew quickly around the harbour and was given the name of King's Town after George III. This name was eventually changed to Kingston, an obvious modification.

The government store was situated at the lower end of Store Street (now Princess Street) and was surrounded by houses and other businesses. Trading furs, agriculture, and imported commodities gave rise to a warehouse district and a busy harbour.

The Herchemers were a United Empire Loyalist family who built a large two-storey home across from the waterfront and docks on the present site of the Prince George Hotel. Their youngest daughter Lily was beautiful and impressionable and she caught the fancy of one of those lonely sailors. Infatuation leads young girls down different paths and Lily and her sailor made a tryst. Her parents were not impressed. Lily was forced into a clandestine affair with her mariner. Secrecy was paramount.

Lily hung a lantern in her window for her lover. It was a signal of safety for their romantic exchange. It was a dangerous game back then, love could cost a sailor his life.

The Prince George Hotel as it looks today.

On one such night Lily fell asleep with her lantern in the window. A sudden gust of wind blew the flames into her room and she perished in the fire. Such a tragic ending for a sweet young girl!

Lily's restless spirit seems to have remained behind, however. She is still there today in what is now the Prince George Hotel. She looks at the ships anchored offshore in the harbour and tied up at the dock. Is she still signalling to her lover?

Lawrence Herchemer died in 1819, and he willed the house to his wife Elizabeth. When Elizabeth passed away in 1840 her son-in-law, John McPherson, turned the building into shops, warehouse space and he leased space to a few saloon owners. Farmers and cityfolk alike came by train and boat for the pleasures that could be had there.

Not everybody appreciated what they saw in Kingston. In 1833, a British visitor wrote "… of the lower orders it is impossible to speak favourably. They have all the disagreeable qualities of the Americans, with none of that energy and spirit of enterprise, which often converts a bad man into a useful citizen. They are sluggish, obstinate, ignorant, offensive in manner, and depraved in morals, without loyalty and without religion."

In 1848 a fire struck three businesses located in the building. William Simpson's saloon, which was situated where the Tir Nan Og, an Irish Pub is today, was partly saved.

Over the years the Prince George Hotel has undergone several facelifts. It has been known as the Herchemer property, the John McPherson House, the New Stone Block, the Oregon Saloon and the Hotel Iroquois. A hotel has operated on this site since Confederation. It has been the Prince George Hotel since 1918, and was in the Herchemer family until 1951.

The grain elevators and wharves that line the harbour are mere shadows of Kingston's waterfront past. The factories and the railroads have yielded their places in history and been replaced by modern hotels, and other tourist attractions. In the park across the street rests the "Spirit of Sir John A.," a refurbished Canadian Pacific train engine. The Visitor Welcome Centre located on Ontario Street across from the Prince George Hotel was once the train station.

In 1978 architect Lily Inglis was hired by the owner of the hotel, Patrick Rousseau, to remodel the building. Is it a coincidence that her name was Lily. The Victorian porch and central tower were reconstructed, lounges were built and the hotel rooms refurbished.

Terminal Properties Limited is the current owner of the Prince George Hotel. This 26-room hotel is one of Kingston's more unique accommodation alternatives. The first floor of the hotel houses Tir Nan Og, an authentic Irish Pub, and Monte's Cigar and Martini Lounge. The third floor is a stomping ground for the still-present spirit of Lily Herchemer. She has survived many owners and outstayed all the guests! And all for a lover that will never return — or will he?

Sean Bravakis works as a desk clerk at the Prince George Hotel and was quite willing to share his stories about Lily. "We have had a number of guests staying overnight who have seen her. What they see is a shadowy form drifting through the hallways of the hotel.

"One member of our cleaning staff was cleaning the rooms on the third floor one afternoon, when something very odd occurred. She cleaned all the rooms on the floor, and locked the doors behind her. When she came out of the last room (310) and started walking down the hall, she heard one by one, the locks turn in each of the doors down the hall behind her. She went back to check and found that each of the doors had been unlocked.'"

Room 310 in the hotel is the same area Lily's original room once was. Two windows now overlook the City Hall and Market Square. When Lily was alive City Hall had not yet been built. Her view was clear to the harbour. Some people say she occupies room 304, but what they don't know is that the room numbers were changed and room 304 became room 310.

An elderly couple, booked into room 310, frantically phoned Sean at the front desk. "They were sleeping in one of the two double beds in the room. The couple awoke to see the second double bed levitating three feet off the floor. The gentleman wanted to know if this was normal!"

According to Sean, "The tower light has been found to be on at night. This is strange because we never turn that light on. One of the owners went to the third floor to check the electrical panel. They found that the breaker for the tower light was in the off position!"

"One day Sharman Howes, our hotel manager, and I were confronted by a couple who had been staying in room 310 with their children. The husband said to us, 'Do you have ghosts here?' He went on to explain that a ghost had interfered with his dream time." It would seem that Lily had visited the gentleman in his dreams.

A female was seen attempting to open room 206 but she simply vanished into thin air without ever entering the room. It seems most ghosts have an affinity for or an ability to use keys.

One day Sean checked some guests into room 311. He took the keys from the key board and proceeded to the room with their luggage. On the way he stopped on the second floor to check the ice machine, one that services both the second and third floors. When he reached room 311, he did not have the keys with him. He retraced his steps, to check beside the ice machine on the second floor; he even searched inside the machine, but to no avail. In frustration he returned to the front desk only to discover the keys to room 311 hanging on the key board. How could that be?

One night the hotel doorman was working on a carpentry project in the basement of the building. The basement stairs are located at the back of the kitchen. It was between three and four o'clock in the morning. To his surprise and alarm, he heard someone coming down the basement stairs. Leaving his work he went to investigate but found no one there.

A clairvoyant visited the hotel lobby in April 1997. She and her friend decided to stay for lunch in the Irish Pub. While eating her meal her attention was drawn to a picture of the Herchemer family hanging over the fireplace. She informed Sean that she had received a message from the photograph. The message was that the spirits there are not happy.

Sean gave her account little thought. After all there was nothing he could do. Later the same day the woman discovered two other pictures of the Prince George Hotel that hang in the stairwell leading to the second floor. The two pictures are hung along with two newspaper articles concerning the Prince George Hotel. Spirits were visible to her in both photos. Apparently Lily has some company!

Sean describes what the woman said, "I see a nun in a white habit holding a book in the front window the Irish Pub. In the second picture, a man with a beard can be seen standing in the lobby window."

With that I proceeded to the stairwell to study these two pictures for myself. To my surprise I could see a faint white form that could pass for a nun with an object in her hands, standing in the pub window. Somehow the photographer had caught this image on film. Then I gazed at the next picture. With a little squinting I could just make out the form of a man with a beard standing in front of the lobby window.

It seems that ghosts are seldom on their own in these public places. If they are all from different times they may be totally unaware of one another and perhaps quite unaware of present-day folks. To them we may only be as clouds drifting by them as they linger, suspended, in time.

A Haunted Farmhouse

~ Creemore ~

RUTH HUGHES LIVES ON A 100-ACRE FARM IN THE SCENIC, ROLLING hills of Creemore, Ontario. When you first meet Ruth, you might think she wouldn't have the time of day for spiritual manifestations — too pragmatic to entertain any "bumps in the night"! Ruth, however, defies first impressions.

Ruth's life is simple in an old-fashioned way. She takes time every day to jot down her experiences and has been keeping this journal for more than thirty years. Perhaps this accounts for the clarity of her mind, not cluttered by unnecessary information. Her acute ability to define experience has allowed her the opportunity to see beyond the veil of death. What does she see?

In 1971 Ruth and her husband, Bill, moved to the countryside of Creemore to live an alternative lifestyle. Ruth had been raised on a farm in the district and knew the joy of such a life. Bill, on the other hand, had no farm experience. Together they purchased a 100-acre farm.

The old homestead, built circa 1860, was in a state of disrepair. Old Peter Giffen had lived out his bachelor years on this farm. For some reason Peter had never found a woman to share his life. Peter's parents, not the original owners, had left the farm to him. He was, by any terms, quite eccentric. Instead of occupying the whole farmhouse, he chose to live in the summer kitchen only. He lived his entire life without electricity or indoor plumbing. During the cold winter months he would huddle by his woodstove for warmth and when his wood supply ran out he slept the night in the barn with the animals for warmth.

Peter had a head for figures. It has been said that he held several of his neighbours' mortgages. The locals told Ruth and Bill that Peter never kept his money in a bank but instead hid his money in the hollow of an apple tree by the barn. At the time Ruth and Bill purchased the farm, the apple tree was gone. Other people said his money was buried in the dirt floor of the basement. The Hughes spent some time digging around the basement, but only found several old green beer bottles. Some people say when he died in his 80s, he was worth more than $250,000.

Peter was a short man with a stocky build and a round face. People commented on his neat appearance; they overlooked the holes in his overalls that exposed his rear end. After all, Peter had no one to look after his domestic needs.

About 1960 Peter became ill and his neighbours drove him to their house and gave him a hot bath. He was later hospitalized for a short time and then moved to a home for the aged. Peter never wanted to leave his farm. He died the same year without the privilege of seeing his farm for one last time.

The unexplained or unusual activity began shortly after the Hughes family moved onto the farm in 1971. Thanks to the journals kept by Ruth no incident went unrecorded!

Shortly after they moved into the farmhouse the Hughes family installed electricity and indoor plumbing. The night the plumbing was completed the toilet flushed continuously. Peter, presumably, was quite taken with the new fixture!

Ruth first "saw" Peter in 1974. She got up one morning and was shocked to see him in her bedroom, sitting in one of the chairs staring out the east window of the house. "He had on a black cap, dark overalls and a jacket. He disappeared when I blinked." Ruth recognized him because she had known Peter when he was alive.

One night in 1974 Bill and Ruth were awakened by footsteps coming down the stairs. At that time their bedroom was located at the bottom of the staircase. "When the footsteps stopped, we experienced a rush of cold air."

Bill and Ruth were convinced they had invisible help harvesting their first grain crop. "We placed the crop in the granary. The next day we discovered that several cedar stakes had been placed standing up in the pile of grain. We had no idea who placed them there nor why. We found out later that in the old days cedar stakes were used to determine the temperature of the grain. If the stakes are pulled out and found to be damp, the grain needs to be turned over to avoid a heat build-up." Ruth says that she knows that Peter placed the stakes in the grain in order to show them how it should be done!

Their dog, Josie, a German shepherd/husky, never liked to go into the barn, especially at harvest time. In 1990 their daughter, Karen, saw Peter in the stable peering into what was once his horse's stall.

Ruth maintains that Peter is not the only ghost living at the farm. "One night when I was in the bathroom I looked up and saw a short, stout woman looking back at me. She had on a long black dress with covered buttons going from the shoulder to hem. I was so annoyed that someone was in my bathroom, that I hauled off and hit her. My fist went right through her and I have not seen her since."

Bill lost his rotary sander and could not find it anywhere. Then one day it appeared on the work bench in his shop. In May 1984 a hand trowel went missing and turned up, later, on top of some jars in the cellar.

One morning the family left the house to feed their herd of goats. When they arrived at the barn they discovered that the goats had already been fed. On another occasion they found the water tap turned on in the barn. The water intake pipe located in the cellar of the house was turned off twice in a short span of time.

In 1986 the electric alarm clock in the bedroom was set and the alarm button pulled out. In the same year the lights in the barn were turned on frequently, when no one was there. One morning Ruth was cooking breakfast when a glass loaf pan flew off the shelf near the stove. "I told whoever did it to stop fooling around."

In 1991 their daughter, Karen, was alone in the house when the doors suddenly opened and closed on their own.

Ruth's mother passed away in 1989. Born and raised a Baptist in Creemore, her mother maintained her strong religious beliefs throughout her life. Ruth explained what happened at the funeral. "We had to invite a Baptist minister from Collingwood to conduct the service. He was rather new at officiating at a funeral. During his sermon he went on and on, talking about death. He even asked us if we were all ready to die. The poor minister couldn't stop. Then it happened — the flowers on top of my mother's coffin flew off the casket. No doubt she was commenting on the minister's address."

Tragically, Bill died on February 28, 1993, after a battle with cancer. The family were devastated. Bill had been bitter about his illness and was not ready to leave when he died. According to Ruth, "Before Bill died he said he wanted to see one of his daughters married and see his first grandson. We were both always interested in reincarnation. We often talked about it. We decided to leave a sign if one of us went first. We never discussed this during his illness, though."

On March 1, 1993, the day after Bill's death, the radio was heard playing in his workshop. A few days later, March 19, Karen's daughter, Amanda, said she saw her grandfather in her bedroom. At 4:00 p.m. that day the shop radio was turned on again.

An old friend of Bill's, Don Jardine, had an experience on April 11 of that year. Don was watching television when the kitchen and living room lights went off. He went downstairs to check the fuse box and discovered that one fuse had been unscrewed.

A month later, on April 16, Ruth discovered that the tools stored in the tractor had been moved and used. The tools were standing in an upright position in the tool box and the lid was open. Five days later their daughter, Peg, had a "dream." She dreamed that the family had built a cabin at the back of the farm. According to Peg, "We were looking through a window and Dad was saying, 'I've found the pathway.' A path was glistening. Dad pointed out the Indian Trail, the one he and Mom had always looked for."

Ruth said to me, "Peg was never aware that Bill and I always wanted to build a cabin back there nor did she know anything about the trail once used by the Native Peoples."

Their daughter, Karen, and son-in-law, Ian, lived in the house next to the farm and had had their own fair share of otherworldly experiences. In July 1993, Ian reported that he heard someone hammering blocks under the beam that supported the hay floor in the barn. Later Ian learned from Ruth that Bill did this task every year.

The same year Karen discovered that a set of plans for a Model T Ford model car had been removed from a cupboard and placed on a table. Ruth had the explanation for this, "Bill always wanted this model, but died before it came out."

On July 28, 1993, Ruth retired to bed for the night. It was her wedding anniversary and it had been a difficult day. She thought of Bill often during that day. Sometime in the night she awakened to see, first, a white light and then, Bill, at the end of her bed. Bill was holding a vase that contained a single, long-stemmed red rose. He had not forgotten!

Ruth experienced a great deal of spiritual activity on January 8, 1994. She found the radio on in the shop again. She would shut the radio off and in a short time it would come on again. The tool box was again left open on the tractor. Ruth also heard banging going on in the storage shed. This continued for three days.

On February 1, 1994, Karen was driving home in her father's old van when she suddenly realized she had a passenger — her father. At the time she had a cup of coffee set in a recessed area of the van. The cup suddenly flew across the van. Ruth recalled that Karen would drive her father down south for his cancer treatments. "Karen often liked to stop halfway to get a cup of coffee, Bill used to say, 'If you are one minute late leaving you won't have time to stop and get a coffee.'"

That same month Ruth recorded in her diary a different "visitor." This time a stockily built man appeared in the house. He was wearing a wine-coloured shirt. Ruth struck the ghost and he left.

During the month of December 1994, Karen misplaced her driver's license. She had no idea where it could have gone. A few days later she found it in her chest of drawers in her bedroom.

In September 1996, Ruth dreamed that she and Bill were walking to Creemore. She felt it was more than a dream. She and Bill had made that walk many times before!

A baby was heard crying in Peg's house in Barrie in November 1996.

There was no baby but Peg watched the cradle rock back and forth on its own. She tied it so it wouldn't move, but it continued to rock. Peg's husband, Bob, also heard a man cooing to a non-existent baby in the night.

In January 1997, Karen dropped a pepper shaker behind her stove. She left it there for the moment and later discovered it sitting on top of her microwave oven.

Bill appeared to Ruth again in April of that year. "He was wearing overalls. He looked well. I saw him upstairs looking out the window. I wanted to talk to him, but before I could, he was gone."

In August he appeared again. Ruth described the experience, "It's a white light that first appears. Then my husband walks through the light. He disappears the moment he walks back into the light. This time Bill came to talk to me about his mother. I could hear his voice in my head. At the time Bill's mother was experiencing some difficulties."

Ruth and her family have found that the spiritual activity is more frequent on birthdays and anniversaries. One thing is certain — they all agree that Bill has remained behind with his family.

In January 1998, the radio in Peg's son's room was turned on. Peg had placed a radio in his room to help him sleep at night. During the evening the radio changed stations three times to country music. Bill had always enjoyed this type of music.

In the spring of 1998 Ruth had problems with the sump pump in the basement. "The pump had ice in it. I unplugged the pump and went upstairs. Some time later I returned to find the pump running and all the ice gone."

That April family and friends gathered to celebrate Ruth's birthday. While everyone was sitting around the room talking, the stereo came on by itself. Everyone looked surprised — except the immediate family! Later that month Karen went to the barn and saw that a pitchfork had been removed from its secure place and shoved in the hay. She could not pull it out.

It would certainly seem that Bill has been unable to leave his family. Bill seems to still be working the farm and enjoys visiting his daughters. One time he appeared with a cousin in tow, one who had died back in the 1940s. A relative in Alberta has reported some activity on his farm — someone had done their barn chores and had let the sheep out to pasture in the early morning before they were up! Perhaps Bill's anger over his early death prevented him from reaching the other side but has allowed him some greater travel.

As for Peter Giffen, he still seems quite attached to the house and property, and he was denied his final wish — to die on his farm.

In 2007 I returned to visit Ruth Hughes. A lot has happened during the past nine years. Ruth herself appeared more transparent. Her connection to the spirit world was quite evident. It would seem she is much closer to the spirit world than the last time we met. Her daughter, Karen, who at the time lived next door with her husband and two daughters, now resides in a new addition attached to her mother's house. Karen's husband died a few years ago, leaving her to raise the girls. Like her mother, Karen is able to communicate with the spirit world.

I was hoping that Karen would share her perspective regarding her mother's experiences with her dead father. I was not to be disappointed. In fact, our meeting was a highly personal, sensitive, and trusting time.

Karen began, "A month ago, I was at a friend's house. I went to bed and just lay there thinking. Suddenly I felt someone put their arm around my waist. Then a young man appeared. His hair was dark. He was in his twenties. He placed both hands on my face and asked me who he was. Then he visually disappeared, but he was still in the bed with me. Then I felt the bed go up and down as he left. That was it."

"When my dad died he came to me. He took me to this white room or space. It was so peaceful. All I could see was white light. There was a hallway too. I didn't want my father to leave. He told me he had to go, and that I would be fine — not to worry. Then I woke up in my bed."

I asked Karen to explain more about this white space. She qualified her statement. "When I leave my body I travel to this room without walls or furniture. It's just a white space."

Karen continued to share a very personal and intimate experience. "I lost my son. He was only nine days old. It was in 1988. I never got to hold him. Matthew was his name.

"Shortly after Matthew's death my great-great-grandmother Betty Hollingworth appeared and took me to this white space — this peaceful white area. My great-great-grandmother manifested a wicker rocking chair. She was seated in it and was holding Matthew. Then she stood up and handed Matthew to me. I sat down in the chair with him.

He was still a baby. I got to hold my baby. I got to hold my son. Then I woke up.

"It usually takes me a couple of days to remember everything."

Her experience with her son didn't end there.

"I saw Matthew again. This time he was about age four. He has appeared to me every year since 1992, always at the end of September near the time of his birthday, although he didn't come last year. He has appeared in front of my daughter Krista too. One time I saw him in the dining room. He was standing there with a fishing rod and a tackle box."

Karen then talked about a close friend and companion who died suddenly two years ago.

"We had always planned to build a house together. Then he died. A year after his death I left my body during sleep. I met my friend in a beautiful meadow where a lovely house was under construction. He was building the house for the two of us. He always loved gardens. The place was full of gardens. The home was situated on a hill surrounded by flowers.

"I saw the porch and the house. The building was a soft yellow and the porch was painted white.

"He still comes to visit me twice a year. He has been in my new home twice. I wake up and there he is looking at me and smiling.

"The first time I saw him it was 2:00 a.m. in the morning. I was watching television. He appeared on the ceiling. I said 'what are you doing on the ceiling?' I feel so good when I see him. He never believed in the spirit world."

According to Karen's daughter, Amanda, her mother's close friend likes to play with the grandchild's toys in the middle of the night. Amanda added, "You can hear the toys running. The lights turn on and off. You get a funny feeling and then you can't sleep."

Karen disclosed information about events that happened in their location here in the past. There could very well be a portal or entranceway to the spirit world here.

Karen continued, "There has been so much death around us. A woman lost control of her car and careened onto the front lawn; an explosion followed and she died in the fire; a few years ago a young boy died in a tractor accident just down the road near my old farmhouse; a neighbour nearby committed suicide."

A native teacher and friend of mine stated that because this is one of the oldest families in the district, the women, not the men, have been given the responsibility of maintaining this portal where spirits can cross between worlds. This is why all the women can see these spirits.

The family have experienced the television going off and on. The DVD player seldom works right. The lights turn off and on and often continue to do so all night. Amanda stated, "I have had to get up in the night and remove my child's toys from the room because they operate on their own. They still continue to run outside the room."

Ruth's husband Bill seems to be quite protective of his great granddaughter. Amanda explained, "Three months ago my child was sleeping in the room with me. I woke up in the night to see my grandfather leaning over the crib and looking at my daughter. Then he disappeared."

Amanda shared a very scary experience that happened to her in 2003 when she was graduating from elementary school.

"After graduation I was in bed asleep when I was suddenly awakened by an odd noise. It sounded like someone was rustling through my papers. The noise wouldn't stop. I became quite scared and screamed out loud for my mother." Karen added, "I rushed to my daughter's room and turned on the light. I quickly removed her from the room. I went back in the room. The light was still on. I wanted whoever or whatever it was out of my house. Then the lamp went flying off the night stand without unplugging. Next a book travelled in mid-air across the room. Then all was quiet. It had left. Amanda has never slept in that room since. The room has remained quite cold. It was a very frightening experience."

Karen's other daughter, Krista, encountered her own dead father two years ago.

"I was in grade six at the time. It had been a bad day. I was quite emotional at the time. I was in bed when I felt someone was there watching me. When I turned over he was there. I looked at him and said 'Dad you're dead, you need to leave.'"

Krista has had another visitor at night.

"The odd night I have awakened to see a young red-headed boy. He appears by my bedside. It is my dead brother Matthew. One night he spoke to me. He said that everything was going to be alright."

It was time to question Ruth. She had been sitting quietly listening to her daughter and her grandchildren speak. I was curious to see if she was still seeing her dead husband, Bill.

Ruth began, "He still comes about the time of our wedding anniversary and my birthday. In death he gets the right date, unlike what he did in life.

"I once saw him smoking in the bedroom, something he did not do when he was alive.

"He usually appears wearing a red and blue plaid shirt, the one my sister made him, and green work pants. He now has a couple of lady spirits with him. I once caught the one lady, who has long, blond, curly hair, sitting on my bed.

"Bill and I had a pact that if he went first and brought a woman to our bed. I would haunt him."

Ruth has had other visitors. This may well be connected to this spiritual portal which exists here.

"I often see little girls now. One is native and the other white. The white girl has blonde hair and appears wearing an old-fashioned green dress. I see her in the front window. She is waving at me. The native girl appears by my stove. I never get to see their faces.

"A native man often appears in broad daylight in my house. He has on a dark overcoat. Then he disappears in a flash." And the story continues …

Some of the spirits in the farmhouse remain a mystery. Who are they? Where did they go? Is there really a dimensional door here on the farm? These questions cannot be answered definitely.

What we do know for certain is that Ruth Hughes is able to see the spirit world. Her detailed accounts provide us with a different viewpoint concerning death. The spiritual activity she has experienced is very real to her. She is determined to help Bill reach the other side, "I keep telling Bill that he should go and have eternal rest."

Nevertheless, Bill has continued to remain near Ruth, their daughters, and now their grandchildren. As of April 2007, according to Ruth and her daughter Karen, Bill is still around keeping a watchful eye over his family and the property, and he is not alone!

The Guild Inn

~ Toronto ~

NEAR THE SCENIC SCARBOROUGH BLUFFS AMID LANDSCAPED GARDENS, monuments, architectural pieces, and original sculptures stands a two-storey château called the Guild Inn.

On the surface, the Guild Inn once celebrated beauty, leisure, and the spirit of creativity. Beneath the surface there is a mystery — an underground maze that guards the secrets of the decades within its dark passages. These secrets are only hinted at by the eerie and unexpected "shadows" that make themselves known to those who dare to enter. When did the mystery begin?

Colonel Harold Child Bickford and his family built a summer residence, a pseudo-Georgian château, here in 1914. The original building had it all: servants' quarters, a nursery, a wing for guests, and plenty of elegance. He called his new home Corycliffe.

In 1921, Bickford sold the property to Father J.M. Fraser of the China Mission College. It was Father Fraser's dream to train missionaries here, who would be subsequently sent to for China. In a very short time Father Fraser attracted more missionary students than he could accommodate.

He sold the Mission College to Mr. Richard Veech Look, an American businessman, in 1923 for the sum of $50,000. It was renamed Cliff Acres until Mr. Look moved on in 1927.

The property remained vacant until 1932, when a widow named Rosa Breithaupt Hewetson purchased it.

At age 44, Rosa embarked on a new project and a new marriage at Cliff Acres. Rosa and her new husband, Spencer Clark, created what they called a "Guild of All Arts," The Guild Inn.

The Clarks hoped to make a contribution in those difficult depression years by stimulating interest in the arts and crafts and by teaching new ways to generate a livelihood. Within a year, there were shops and studios dedicated to sculpture, batik, hand-loom weaving, tooled leather, ceramics, pewter and copper, wrought-iron, and woodwork.

During the winter of 1942–43, the Clarks were asked by the Canadian government to vacate the entire premises, and the Guild Inn became an official naval base where the first group of Women's Royal Naval Service (WRENS) were trained.

The whole complex was renamed H.M.C.S. *Bytown II* during the military occupancy, and was used to train 50 WRENS as radio operators. The main inn itself was occupied by top military brass.

During the war, Dr. Clarence Hincks, head of the Canadian Council of Mental Hygiene, went to England to visit and evaluate a unique hospital called Mill Hill where patients were treated for nervous disorders. Upon his return to Canada, he persuaded the government to create this type of facility for its own veterans, and from 1944 to 1947, the Guild Inn became a hospital known as Scarborough Hall.

The Clarks were given back their property in 1947. But what about the tunnels? When were they built?

Let us explore the mystery. The first house was built in 1914 by a military man and sold soon after World War I. The property was taken over during World War II by the Canadian military. Who built the tunnels, and why? What was the military really up to at the Guild during the war?

The Guild Inn, just prior to being closed in 2001.

One tunnel extended just beyond the property to Lake Ontario, perhaps in order to provide secret access or egress from the Guild. This would not have been the first time the military had constructed such tunnels on a lakeshore property in Ontario. For example, no one living in Oshawa during World War II was aware of Camp X, a secret agent training camp. It, too, had a series of buildings connected by underground tunnels linked to Lake Ontario.

The people employed there were sworn to secrecy. Possibly, the answer to all this still lies hidden beneath the ground of the Guild.

Krystal Leigh, a paranormal researcher and field investigator who once lived on the grounds of the Guild, recalled, "My grandmother talked about working here after the war. She said the tunnels extended all around the property. A sliding bookshelf located in Corycliffe led to the basement and a tunnel."

Whatever went on in the tunnels, whether it was espionage, top secret medical experiments, or simply offices hidden underground to prevent detection, the air was bad, it was dark, and the energy was heavy. And that energy imprint has remained.

When the Clarks regained their home in 1947 some of the former crafts people returned as well. The Guild's guests and visitors came back

Ornate entranceway situated in the Guild Inn gardens.

in even larger numbers. It was necessary to expand the accommodations and the Guild Inn's reputation grew once more.

The grounds of the Guild are still adorned with a collection of historic architectural features. More than 40 years of effort by Spencer Clark resulted in the preservation of fragments of approximately sixty buildings; items like Sir Frederick Banting's fireplace and the original steps of Osgoode Hall are here. A grindstone made in Ireland circa 1860 that was brought to Canada by the Goldie family of Galt is also on the grounds of the inn.

Spencer was so concerned with preserving Toronto's heritage buildings that he became instrumental in saving Old City Hall from demolition. The grounds of the Guild are literally a monument to his efforts.

Carole Lidgold described the last years of the Clarks at the inn. "In 1975 at the age of 87 Rosa had a stroke. She was confined to a wheelchair after the stroke and was no longer able to participate as fully in the activities of the inn. Spencer suffered from crippling arthritis. He and Rosa knew that their years of owning and managing the inn were coming to a close.

"For ten years Spencer tried to convince the government of Ontario and Metropolitan Toronto to buy the property. In a statement to the press he said, 'Before I die I want to make sure this place is going to continue. It's my life's work.'"

In May 1978 Metropolitan Toronto council voted to purchase the property. Mel Lastman, later mayor of Toronto (1997–2003), voted against the purchase.

On July 13, 1981, at the age of 93, Rosa Breithaupt Hewetson Clark died. Spencer died of a heart attack on February 11, 1986.

Until the late fall 2001, the Guild Inn remained open and served as an overnight destination, dining facility, and wedding reception centre. Change is now in the wind for the Guild.

Although the original château, or main building, is an historic site, other buildings may be torn down for the future development of a lavish resort. All the items in the inn were labelled for auction. Fortunately, I did tour the grounds and buildings before any demolition or the auction sales took place.

On September 16, 2001, Krystal Leigh, Sue Darroch, Annette Goodrich, Dee Freedman, and Steve Dietrich of Hauntings Research Group and their associate Lisa Reid entered the tunnel system of the Guild Inn to conduct an investigation of paranormal activity.

Sue recounted, "Steve and I entered the tunnel. The lighting was poor, furnished solely by our flashlight. I immediately pointed out to Steve that I believed there was something in the far corner. It appeared to be a dark, huddled, human-like mass. Annette and Dee entered this room and both immediately and almost in unison stated that there was an 'entity' in the same corner. While Dee maintained her composure, Annette was physically and emotionally shaken by the unfolding experience and had started to cry.

"Then my eyes were drawn to an area directly behind Lisa and Krystal. I saw what appeared to be movement, as if someone had entered the tunnel area and was coming toward us. This movement stopped just short of Lisa. As my attention had become solely focused on this new event, I did not notice the apparent departure of the entity in the far corner. Whatever it was that had approached us in the tunnel, it was my feeling that it was still there as we left the area."

Dee Freedman, while subsequently staying at the inn, encountered some uninvited company in her room. "After attending an anniversary party, some of us booked rooms at the Guild Inn for the night. A few of us ended up talking the night away instead of going to bed. At about 5:30 a.m. we heard a loud banging from the room next door. We thought that we might be disturbing our neighbour. As we continued to talk, the doorknob between the suites turned and I said, 'What are they trying to do, get into our room?' at which we all laughed. We later found out that the couple staying in that room had heard the same banging and thought it was us."

By 6:30 a.m. they decided to retire. It was then that Dee encountered a presence. "As I lay down and closed my eyes, a little boy approached me and placed himself right in front of my face. He really wanted my attention and I could not help but notice his unusual eyes — one was brown and the other was blue.

"I was so exhausted that I told him to go away. I immediately fell asleep until 9:00 a.m. At that time I went across the hall to another room to join the group. While I was sipping my coffee, I described the visit from the little boy earlier that morning. When I mentioned his eyes, I thought one of the girls was going to faint. She said a resident had been having dreams about a little boy with one blue eye and one brown eye."

For several years, the inn closed for the winter months. Krystal Leigh, her husband, and young son resided in the inn alone during the winter. They were hired to monitor the grounds and buildings. On February 16, 2002, I joined Dee Freedman, Krystal Leigh, Patrick Cross, and Steve Dietrich at the Guild Inn. It was my intention to interview the group and tour the tunnels.

We gathered in a suite on the fourth floor of the inn. We seated ourselves around a coffee table in the living room. Krystal shared her family history and attachment to the Guild, plus a couple of her encounters with spirits.

Contemporary photo of Guild Inn Gardens. A brick and stone sign welcomes guests to the open-air "Music Hall."

"At one time an employee working in the prep area of the kitchen heard a bang inside the walk-in fridge. The fridge was always locked. When he went to investigate he discovered the lock had been opened. When he opened the door, he discovered that a box of melons had been knocked over. He cleaned up the mess and relocked the door. A short time later he heard another bang. He turned and saw the fridge lock lying on the floor. He locked it again.

"He went back to his work. Suddenly, he felt someone tugging on a towel that was sticking out of his back pocket. He turned around and saw an apparition. It was a man standing by the doorway to his left. He was wearing a top hat and tuxedo with tails. The spirit walked around a table in the kitchen and then went through a closed door. The employee lost sight of him."

Krystal and her family lived on the sixth floor. Krystal had an experience that made her hair stand on end. "I was taking a shower. When I finished, I stepped out and looked at the bathroom mirror. It was fogged up — except for two handprints.

Krystal had other experiences. "My son loved to play with toys. Sometimes you could watch his toys roll across the floor on their own.

"When my son was a baby, I took a picture of him by the Christmas tree. When I had the photograph developed, it showed him and a misty form standing near him by the tree. When I had the photograph enhanced, the form proved to be a little boy wearing a dress, with long hair."

The week before we met in 2002, Krystal had an odd experience. "Last Saturday I found my purse floating in the toilet."

As we were all listening, I felt a cold chill down the back of my spine. The feeling left but returned within seconds. I looked around to see if there was a window open. This was not the case. Then Patrick said, "We have company." I stared at him. The whole group sat still.

Patrick said, "Dee's camera case, on one of the shelves on the bookcases, is moving up and down." It was true. Patrick had pulled out his EMF detector, a device for measuring the electromagnetic field of an area. The needle had started to move erratically back and forth.

Dee said, "We have two spirits in the room with us. One is looking over Terry's shoulder. They are interested in what he is writing." Just as suddenly as they had come, they were gone. On that note, we decided to venture into the tunnels of the Guild Inn.

We took the elevator to the basement. From there we went down a set of stairs into a tunnel. The atmosphere was quite stuffy and heavy. The group remarked how warm it was in the tunnel. Apparently the tunnels are normally cold.

As we walked down the tunnel, Dee caught sight of something running down a side tunnel we had just crossed. I began to look over my shoulder. We entered a small room that contained an old telephone system.

Krystal said, "My mom once saw a female apparition here. She was wearing a navy uniform. She had sharp features with her hair pulled back." Dee sensed something about that apparition and said, "She was a nasty woman. She held a position in the military high command that once occupied the building."

Steve had remained out in the tunnel while we were investigating this room. As we were leaving, he said that he had heard a door close in one of the tunnels. We were not alone.

Historic photo of Guild Inn, date unknown.

We re-entered the tunnel system and walked to another room. Dee and Krystal both said that they felt that corpses might have been kept there. We didn't linger there for long.

It was time to return to daylight. We ascended to the ground level and walked up to the elevator. Krystal pushed the elevator button. It would not stop at the ground floor. Instead it travelled down to the basement to the tunnels. That was odd. We looked at each other. We waited until it returned to the ground floor. Then the door opened. We stepped inside and wondered who else, or what else, was in there with us.

Returning to the Guild Inn in April 2007, I was shocked to see the building all boarded up. The roof was sagging and the paint had begun to peel. The structure looked so abandoned and unloved. This historic place was about to vanish from view.

What was most eerie was the immaculate condition of the grounds. The antique structures from long-gone buildings still adorn the beautiful gardens and lawns. A bride and her bridesmaids had just arrived to take some wedding pictures. A young woman and her daughter strolled the grounds. Did any of them have any idea about the hauntings of the Guild Inn? The answer was no.

I walked up to the mother and her daughter and asked if they knew the fate of this historic site. The mother replied that there was a possibility that the inn was still going to be torn down to make room for a new hotel. I asked her if she had ever heard of the ghost stories surrounding the structure and grounds. She answered no. I explained that she was probably standing above an underground tunnel that housed rooms and secrets. She shuddered at the thought.

Despite several calls I was unable to connect with the city authorities that are in charge of this site. It would seem that the fate of this magnificent setting and its buildings still lies in the hands of the City of Toronto. Perhaps the spirits inhabiting the Guild Inn have something to do with the unresolved direction of this place. They may be content to have the inn closed and to have the entire structure and underground tunnels to themselves.

The Oxford County
Courthouse and Jail

~ Woodstock ~

THE FIRST PERSON TO BE PUBLICLY HANGED FOR MURDER IN WOODSTOCK, Ontario, was Thomas Cook. It happened on Tuesday, December 16, 1862, at 11:00 a.m.

Born in Nottingham, England, Thomas made his way to Canada and settled in Blandford Township, Oxford County, Ontario. He met and married a young woman from a prominent family who lived in the village of Innerkip, near Woodstock. The newlyweds moved to the Township of Blenheim. There Thomas worked as a labourer and they raised three children.

Thomas Cook was a difficult man, well-known to be a womanizer, a braggart, a liar, a drunk, and a fighter. As the years passed he also became lazy, fat, and so dissipated he was unemployable. He and his wife and family moved back to Innerkip to be closer to her people.

In February 1856, Thomas purchased an acre of land and there he built a log shanty. His one and only son died shortly thereafter. Mrs. Cook

Dundas Street in Woodstock around the time Thomas Cook was jailed.

passed away a short time after that and he was now the sole caregiver to his two daughters.

He could no longer cope and his father-in-law saw fit to remove the children from his care. Thomas continued to drink, perhaps even more heavily, and by 1862 had lost enough of his eyesight to be considered clinically blind. However, Thomas was still able to discern light from dark and could travel about with a stick.

Despite his obesity, his drinking, and his blindness, he found a new wife. Her name was Bridget. She was twelve years his junior and she was also an alcoholic.

Together they were the talk of the village. They both relied on charity and would often go begging and panhandling through Innerkip and Woodstock. Local gossip maintained that their constant bickering could be heard a quarter of a mile away.

In spring 1862 the Cooks left the village to journey about the countryside for a few months. On their way home they stopped in Woodstock at the home of their friend, Leonard Clouse. On Sunday night, July 29, 1862, Thomas and Bridget got very drunk and Clouse asked them both to leave.

On Monday morning, Nelson Culver, another friend, left for Innerkip and took Thomas and Bridget with him. On the journey home Thomas and Bridget quarrelled constantly. At one point, she called him a liar and in a fit of rage he screamed, "By the living God, I will murder you tonight." Thomas struck his wife frequently on the drive home. They reached their shanty at about noon.

Nelson Culver explained what happened next, "The Cooks got out of the wagon and went into the house. I went to feed my horse. Afterward Mr. Everet arrived and went into the house to see Cook, and on coming out, and in conversation with me, Cook shut the door. I went afterward to the window, and heard Cook and his wife quarrelling; afterward she went to bed. I left to get some grass for my horse, and on going back to the house, and looking through the window, I saw Cook on his knees, on the bed, having hold of his wife by the throat with one hand, and striking her on the head with a stick. She cried out, 'For God's sake, Tommy, don't kill me.' I hollered out for him to stop, and he grinned his teeth at me, and told me that if I interfered I would get the same. I left the window, and in a short time heard more noise, and I returned to the window. I saw Mrs. Cook cross-ways on the bed, and Cook stooping over her holding her by the throat, and striking her on the face. I again hollered to him to stop. He said, 'Goddamn you, will you take her part?'

"I looked in the window again and he was still beating her. Next he lifted her up, and let her head fall against the logs of the house. I heard her breathing as if blood was gargling in her throat."

Culver then went to seek help. He contacted a Mrs. Ellis and a Miss Dean, but neither of them wished to interfere. Culver then returned to the Cook's shanty.

"At last he opened the door. I saw his hands all covered with blood — his face and clothes were all covered with blood. He asked me if I would take him to Warsaw next morning. I told him I would. I was afraid to speak to him about his wife, lest he might get mad and pitch into me. I made the alarm, but everyone refused to interfere.

"Afterward I went to the village and met Mr. Vincent about six o'clock and told him, and he, along with others, went to the house of Cook. I did not go till next morning, when I saw Mrs. Cook lying on her face on the bed, quite dead. She was washed by this time, but the blood was not all washed off. Dr. Scott held an inquest."

Thomas Cook was arrested, tried in the old Court House adjacent to the jail in Woodstock and found guilty of murder. The sentence and judgment of the court was that "he be taken hence to the place whence he came (Oxford County Jail) and that on Tuesday, the 16th day of December, he will be taken to the place of execution and be hanged by the neck until his body is dead. And may the Lord have mercy upon his soul."

The place of execution was built on the north wall of the jail yard. A few steps led from the inner courtyard to the scaffold which was on a platform approximately nine metres (20 feet) from the ground. About two-thirds of a metre (two feet) from the front, in the centre of the platform, was the "drop." Immediately above this was the beam, in the centre of which was placed a hook, and on the southside of the drop was the bar.

At five minutes of 11:00 a.m., on Tuesday, December 16, 1862, the procession formed in the following order — the sheriff, Mr. James Carroll, in uniform; the deputy, Mr. A. Ross; the executioner; and the condemned, Thomas Cook, with a white cap on his head. The executioner was said to be from the immediate neighbourhood, though it was impossible to recognize him, as he was thoroughly disguised by a large white towel drawn across his mouth and nose, a pair of goggles obscured his eyes, and an old white hat was drawn closely over the goggles.

The *Ingersoll Chronicle* reported the hanging in an article published Friday, December 19, 1862, "Some three thousand four hundred persons were in front and at each side of the scaffold; we regretted to see so many women in attendance.

"The unfortunate man commenced a prayer in the following words, 'My blessed redeemer, come to me now and reclaim my soul!'

"The lever was drawn at exactly eleven o'clock, and the victim passed through the trap; the shock was so great from the fall that his head was completely severed from the body and fell some three feet (one metre) west of the now lifeless trunk. There was no quivering, no convulsion, death was sudden. It was truly a shocking sight to see the blood spouting from the severed arteries. The crowd were amazed, and for a moment no one could realize the fate of the poor old man."

The Woodstock jail as it appears today.

The townspeople would discover his other fate at a much later time. Some people would learn that you can extinguish the life from a body, but how you treat the spirit is another matter. So where did Thomas Cook's spirit go — wait and see!

Moments after the body fell to the ground it was lifted up and placed in a coffin provided for the purpose. The people seemed disappointed that they were prevented from seeing the victim suspended by the neck.

According to the custom of the day, following the execution, a mask was made of the face and attached to the jail wall over the outer door of the jail. It can still be seen there today. It was also the first and last time a mask of this sort was made at the jail. What was the thought behind such a ghoulish custom?

Thomas Cook's remains were given to his friends who proposed that the burial take place in Innerkip. The coffin was placed in a wagon to be conveyed to the village.

In 1862 various methods were employed to secure bodies for dissection and study. Medical men experienced great difficulty in obtaining bodies for research. A hanging would provide an ideal opportunity. Although a necessary part of any doctor's education, at the time it was generally accepted that one's mortal remains must be intact upon burial. In fact, the ignorant and uneducated would be horrified at the idea of "disturbing" the body.

Someone from the Woodstock Medical Clinic, situated at the corner of Finkle and Dundas Streets in Woodstock, approached Cook's friends in the hope of striking a deal to have them hand over his body for dissection. One can guess at the nature of his friendships and at the degree of loyalty his friends had for him. They sold his remains.

Cook's body was deposited in a dissecting room in the clinic. Thomas Cook never received a proper burial, nor did he give his consent to allow his body to be used for science. It is a plausible assumption that he would never have approved.

The old Woodstock courthouse was deemed a fire hazard in the 1880s and a new courthouse was commissioned to be built on the same site in 1888. The old building was completely dismantled.

The County Jail continued to operate and there were four more hangings in Woodstock. In 1890 J.R. Birchall, age 24, was hung for the shooting death of his 24-year-old companion, F.C. Benwell, in a Blenheim Township swamp. Known as Lord Somerset, his trial attracted world-wide attention. Some people say he also haunts the jail.

Norman Garfield was hung for the shooting death of Ben Johnson, a candy store merchant and former wrestler, in a robbery in 1921.

Elizabeth Tilford, at the age of 56, was hung in 1935 for poisoning her third husband by feeding him arsenic over a period of 11 days. One can only wonder at the fate of her first two husbands. She was the first and only woman executed in Oxford County and the eighth woman executed in Canada since Confederation.

In 1954 Velibor Rajik, a Yugoslav immigrant, age 34, was hung for stabbing his landlady, Mrs. Ernest Boyd, to death at a rooming house on Perry Street in Woodstock.

A very old photograph of the Courthouse and in the background the Woodstock Jail.

The first four executions were performed in the exercise yard and the fifth hanging was done inside the jail building. In 1977, the jail was closed for economic reasons. Today the jail houses the Oxford County Board of Health.

In 1903 a work crew, digging in the area where the old medical clinic site once stood, found a skeleton. Their grisly discovery turned out to be Thomas Cook. The bones were removed and buried elsewhere in an unmarked grave.

It was at the time of this discovery that a flurry of ghost sightings was first reported at the jail. A number of prisoners claimed to have seen a shadowy figure in the night. One night, a cellmate named Isaiah Wright began to scream. The guards ran to his cell (number 13) only to find Wright huddled in the corner, shaking and mumbling. After some time he admitted that a ghost had appeared to him three times that night. It would seem that Thomas Cook had returned!

Ever since that time, a ghost, believed to be the ghost of Thomas Cook, has haunted the courthouse and jail. Some people say he occupies the fourth floor of the courthouse, while others seem to think he lurks in the courthouse tower.

The second County Courthouse, completed in 1892, is an impressive pink sandstone building designed by architect R.T. Brookes of Detroit. He was later dismissed when major problems were discovered in the exterior walls. Fowler and Cuthbertson of Woodstock were hired and the original contractor, W.C. Smith of Detroit was fired. When the building was finally completed, the cost was double the original estimate.

A stone-carved monkey gargoyle can be seen at the top of the front gable and other monkey heads adorn the pillar tops. The monkeys do not show up in the original plans and popular belief holds that they were carved for spite when council made a monkey out of the first contractor.

Ernie Hunt, a jack-of-all-trades, as he likes to refer to himself, spearheaded the renovations of the old courthouse in 1980. Ernie was involved in the design and execution of the changes to the building and he has had incredible experiences there.

When Ernie first started the last restoration project, he had no knowledge of the ghost of Thomas Cook. However, in a very short time Thomas introduced himself to Ernie!

Ernie noticed that things would go missing. Each night he would lay out the tools and materials for the next day, "I redid all the plumbing in copper and brass. Some days the fittings would go missing. I always placed my materials on a scaffold. I was working on the third floor of the courthouse when this happened. It was so strange, because the fittings would reappear the next day in the boiler room on the first floor of the courthouse.

"Then we began working on creating an elevator shaft from an old chimney in the building. The chimney itself measured seven feet by eight feet (two and three tenths metres by two and six tenths metres) and was 80 feet (26 metres) in height. We constructed a shaft in the chimney to fit an elevator. Then we built an elevator car operated by a hand control. At night I would gather up all the tools and lay them out on the platform of the elevator car. The entranceway to the elevator shaft was closed off. It was impossible for anyone to gain entry to the shaft and I was always the last person to leave the building at night and the first to arrive in the morning. It wasn't unusual to arrive in the morning and discover a hand trowel or level missing from the elevator car. Once again these tools would reappear in the boiler room. There was no way anyone could have removed those tools from the elevator shaft unless they were a ghost. Once the elevator was installed and certified, we still only used it ourselves for a period of time."

Ernie then described an experience that occurred with the elevator, "I spent a lot of time at night by myself in the courthouse designing and planning the work to be done the next day. One Sunday night I was working late at night and discussing some plans with the County Engineer. We were on the first floor of the building sitting on the interior window ledges, across from the elevator. Suddenly the elevator started up all by itself. We looked at one another in total amazement since there were only two keys made to operate the elevator. The custodians had one key which was kept in the foreman's office and I had the other key. There we were watching the elevator light indicator register floor '2', '3', and '4.'"

"Somehow the elevator had travelled up the shaft and stopped at the fourth floor of the courthouse. We were the only two people in the building. I said to the engineer, 'Where is that thing going?' Then the elevator started up again and travelled to the third floor and then stopped. In a short time it moved to the second floor and stopped. Finally it landed on the first floor, stopped, and the elevator doors opened up right in front of us. I jokingly said, 'Who just got out of the elevator? I didn't recognize him.'

"At the time I thought perhaps the system had a short. So I called a technician the next day and he showed up to report 'no such thing.' You see it is impossible for the elevator to stop at floors unless someone is in the elevator and pushing the buttons! Someone has to physically press the floor button."

Ernie's wife, Yvonne, often joined her husband at night to keep him company. One particular night Ernie was in another part of the building while Yvonne was on the first floor of the courthouse. Once again the elevator started and the doors opened. Then the doors shut. Yvonne ran to find Ernie.

One night the Hunts were sitting on the first floor of the courthouse with their 18-month-old grandson when the elevator turned itself on again. The elevator doors opened suddenly and before they had time to stop him, their grandson ran into the elevator and the doors shut behind him. The elevator made its way up to the fourth floor and stopped.

George Forbes Sr., Gaoler, and John Cameron, Cor. Positioned above an undated photo of the Woodstock County Gaol.

"We could hear our grandson screaming as we watched the elevator light indicate to us that it had just left the fourth floor and stopped on the third floor, without the doors opening. I ran up to the third floor, pushed the button, the elevator came down again from the fourth floor and when the doors opened, I grabbed my grandson from the elevator. It was such a frantic experience. My grandson still remembers that elevator ride to this day."

Passageways do exist beneath the building. Ernie explained that these tunnels had been built to accommodate an air conditioning system. You can imagine how eerie it would be to look down a tunnel when you know Thomas Cook might appear at any time. Well, this did happen — to Ernie.

"We were down in the tunnels one day and caught sight of the ghost. We only saw a misty form outlining a head and shoulders but that was something!"

Ernie could feel the presence of the spirit whenever he was working in the courthouse. He described it as "just a feeling and then every once in awhile you catch something like a shadow go by, out of the corner of your eye." Ernie often felt a tap on the shoulder, but at the time told himself it was just a muscle twitch.

When I toured the courthouse in 1997 before interviewing Ernie Hunt, I had no information about what section of the building Thomas Cook haunted. I visited the first and then second floors of the courthouse and finally found myself on the third floor. The fourth floor is off limits to the public and the only access to it is by a staircase behind a locked door or by way of the elevator. On the third floor I stood in front of the locked door leading to the fourth floor. I stood there for a moment or more and then asked a worker walking by if they knew of the spirit that haunts this building. They did.

I then asked, "Where is the spirit seen most frequently?"

Reply, "Right where you are standing; by the door leading to the fourth floor!"

I thought as much.

Where does the spirit roam according to Ernie Hunt? "I believe Thomas Cook walks the halls of the courthouse of the jail and of the old land registry office on the corner of the property that now houses the historical society."

I journeyed back to Woodstock in May 2007 to find out if Thomas Cook still inhabited the Oxford County Courthouse. It was about 5:00 p.m. when I arrived. I entered the building and proceeded down the first floor hallway. I was hoping to interview anyone I could find. I knew my best bet would be the custodial staff who worked the night shift. I entered one office and asked a female staff if she had ever encountered or heard the ghost of Thomas Cook. She replied that the only unusual activity in the building she had ever experienced were the bats that would occasionally fly through the office or hallway of the structure. She did manage to locate a phone number for the custodial staff. I tried the number, but received no answer. I continued on to the second floor. I then met three ladies working in an office. I asked the same question. They all looked at me with great suspicion. The reply was a curt "no."

I decided to see if I could find any custodians working in the courthouse, but this endeavor failed. No one was to be found to share a story. Not wanting to give up I decided to go outside to my car and sit and wait for a custodian to arrive. As I proceeded down the first-storey hallway I came to the elevator. Just as I walked past the elevator the bell rang and the elevator door opened. I waited but no one came out. I walked back and looked. No one was inside the elevator. I realized that Thomas Cook had just announced his presence. He was still playing with the elevator as he had done with Ernie Hunt. Then the door to the elevator shut. I left the building and proceeded to the parking lot when a woman with whom I had already spoken to stopped in her car and rolled down her window. She said, "You see the man standing over there talking to another person?"

I looked where she pointing to and nodded my head.

She said, "That man is the Reeve of the Township, perhaps he might have a story for you."

I thanked her and approached the Reeve. He was a pleasant man who invited me back into the building to his office. He had no experiences of hauntings in the building, but was very aware of the stories surrounding the ghost of Thomas Cook, including the elevator travelling to floors on its own and opening by itself.

The Reeve thought a co-worker in his office might have a story for me, but unfortunately he had nothing to offer. Disappointed, I headed for the front doors but just as I was about to leave two men greeted me. As they entered the building and from their uniforms I realized they were the custodial staff. When I explained my quest one of them gave me the name of a female co-worker who had stories. He gave me her cell phone number as she was in another building.

Reluctantly and anonymously, she shared her story.

She and another female employee had worked together in the building at night in 2005 and 2006. "We would be working and then hear doors slamming down the hall. When the staff leaves at night they lock the office doors behind them. We would hear a door slam and then go to investigate. We checked all the doors but every one was locked.

"Then we would be working on the first floor and suddenly hear the elevator doors open on their own. It would really freak you out.

"When we worked on the second floor we would gather cardboard boxes up and leave them at the top of the stairs. Later we would just kick them down the stairs to the first floor.

"This one night we heard cardboard boxes being thrown down the stairs. We rushed to the stairs but were no cardboard boxes to be found.

"One evening we were working in the Judge's private quarters on the second floor when we heard a noise down the hallway. My companion went to investigate. I was just about to leave the office when out of nowhere I heard this slamming noise behind me. I was so scared; I bolted out of the room and jumped right over my cleaning cart that was located at the door."

I asked her if she ever heard voices. She replied, "We once heard what we thought were people arguing just outside the building. We went outside to see, but no one was there.

"After working here for a while you wonder if your mind is playing tricks on you. You hear things, but you never see anything."

I asked her if she believed in a spirit or spirits haunting the building. She stated, "I can't answer that question." A period of silence followed. I thanked her for sharing her stories and hung up.

What is it that keeps a spirit behind in this place? Perhaps a death-prayer wasn't answered, a soul not redeemed, Was the violation to his body so traumatic that Cook lingered? The timing seems to indicate that it is indeed his spirit but it could possibly be one of the other four of the condemned. Do our own misdeeds hold us back? You be the judge.

Many say that hell is our own making; perhaps that's what happens when we stick around because of our misdeeds. Something to ponder, isn't it?

The Albion Hotel

~ Bayfield ~

THE HISTORIC VILLAGE OF BAYFIELD, PERCHED ABOVE THE SANDY shoreline of Lake Huron, has a long, strong past. Civic pride is a tradition and the folks in Bayfield are very friendly. During our visit there we had one of the warmest welcomes my wife and I have ever had anywhere. Especially at the Albion Hotel. The Albion Hotel is located on the main street and it feels just like home. The staff are courteous and welcoming.

The structure was built in the 1840s and was designed to be a store. The proprietor, Robert Reid, built an addition in 1856 and the Albion opened its doors as a hotel. Since that time the hotel has catered to the needs of villagers and tourists.

In 1897 it was the scene of a murder.

The village of Bayfield got its start as a port. Rich agricultural land to the east produced valued crops for export and fishing was also a major business. Lake Huron is a beautiful body of water and here was a spot with a natural harbour and a river mouth, ideal for a settlement. The land upon which the village was founded was originally purchased, sight unseen, by Baron van Tuyll van Serooskerken of The Hague. He had been advised to do so by his good friend Admiral Henry Wolsey Bayfield, who had served as a surveyor on the Great Lakes. The settlement took the admiral's name.

Bayfield was laid out on a radial plan with a town square at the hub of the wheel. The main street was at the northwest corner of one of the spokes. By the 1850s the main street was a hub of activity with many shops and businesses. There were half a dozen hotels operating throughout the village and there was an air of abundance.

Unfortunately, it was not to last because of choices made by the railway. The new line by-passed Bayfield and went to Goderich, just a few miles down the Lake Huron shore. Industry withered and died.

The locals were a resourceful lot and soon this picturesque village began to recover. Perhaps the railway did them a favour because, instead of industry, they had tourists and an abundance of lovely summer homes.

The local newspaper in 1895 attested to this, "A few years ago Bayfield was little heard of outside the country; today she is talked of and widely famed as a pleasant and beautiful watering place."

Tourists fell in love with the quaint atmosphere of the village and its beautiful landscape. The trees there are magnificent; even today there is a slippery elm reported to be 560 years old.

Although serene on the surface, as in any community there were secrets, distrust, alcohol abuse, and in this town, even murder. Murder can create a situation in which one or more souls become trapped at the scene of the crime. This, no doubt, explains one aspect of the paranormal activity occurring at the Albion Hotel.

In the 1890s Maria and Edward Elliott were the proprietors of the Albion and it was also their home. The Elliotts had much sorrow in their family. By 1895 they had already buried three sons, the youngest was only 14 years old and the eldest was 28.

Maria, her daughter, Lily, and her two remaining sons, Fred and Harvey, shared the daily chores at the hotel. It was well known that Harvey had an argumentative nature and became worse when he drank.

On November 8, 1897, 21-year-old Harvey and a friend, Dumart, went out drinking in nearby Varna, a village located six and a half kilometres (four miles) from Bayfield.

Albion Hotel as it appears today.

About 8:30 p.m. Harvey and Dumart returned home to the Albion. It didn't take too long for Harvey to have another drink in the bar, now the dining room, and then to quarrel with his 19-year-old brother, Fred. There was trouble brewing. The boys left the bar.

Fred was standing outside the hall door. Harvey was standing on the platform in front of the hotel. Then he shouted to Fred, "Go into the house."

George Erwin, a witness to the events, stated that he heard Harvey swearing at his brother. Harvey was in a temper. George and Lily tried to restrain him from striking Fred. Lily screamed for help.

The family knew that the brothers were not in the habit of quarrelling except when Harvey had been drinking. Mrs. Elliot rushed to Fred to talk to him. Harvey was only a few feet away when someone caught sight of a revolver in Fred's hand. Fred then shouted, "Keep him away from me or I'll shoot him."

Suddenly Harvey charged Fred; Fred raised the gun and it went off. Harvey fell into his friend's arms. The bullet had passed through his trachea.

Fred stood still for a moment and then tears welled up in his eyes. He had shot his own brother. Although it was not in the newspaper accounts, it was rumoured that they tried to get Harvey to the water pump for a drink before they took him inside.

Harvey was eventually carried into the bar, where he died within seconds. His blood permanently stained the wooden floor.

Fred was tried for murder. The locals took up a petition for clemency but the jury returned a tough verdict: "Guilty; with a strong recommendation to mercy."

The judge sentenced Fred to several years in the Kingston Penitentiary. He was released early due to poor health. He died on September 13, 1905, at the age of 28.

As for Harvey, it seems he has remained at the place of his death.

Although there have been no visual sightings to confirm the identity, someone likes to turn a light on at night in the bar area after the hotel has closed for the night. Someone likes to flip a beer tap on occasion, too. Psychics have confirmed a male presence in the new dining area.

Kim Muszynski talks about the Albion. Upon his return from the West, where he had worked for Delta Western, he went out with his family for lunch at the Albion Hotel in Bayfield. Today he owns it.

"I never heard any stories of a haunting until we began some renovation work downstairs."

The renovations involved moving the original bar from the left side of the entranceway, to the right side. Kim then turned the old bar area into an old-fashioned dining room furnished with simple antiques.

The present-day bar is a very friendly place. Copper-topped tables of all sizes and miscellaneous chairs furnish the area. A gas fireplace is both warm and atmospheric. In the former years this room was a gathering-place and had a player piano.

It was during renovations that Kim encountered his first indication of paranormal activity. "We finished the work downstairs and were just getting started upstairs. I had hired a painter who said that he didn't paint unless there was music playing. So we provided him with a portable stereo. We had all just started working when the radio went off on its own. This happened three times for no apparent reason."

Kim was not convinced the hotel was haunted — but that soon changed. "One night my partner, John, who was sleeping in the next room upstairs in the hotel, came into my room twice. He had heard his name being called. He thought I had called him, but I hadn't. On the second occasion, just when I was about to drift off to sleep, I felt a hand touch my face. I didn't sleep for the rest of the night."

Nancy had been a young woman who married a local farmer by the name of John. The odd thing was that she never went to live with her husband. Instead, she lived at the Albion Hotel in the room that Kim had used as a bedroom and which is now the common room. Her husband visited the hotel to be with her. Nancy lived there until she died. Perhaps she still calls his name in the night, "John!"

There has been activity over the years, particularly during any renovations, but it had been quiet in the last few months; that is, until I made an appointment for an interview.

The night before I arrived, Kim had a very unusual experience at his home. "I have two dogs. When I went to feed them I took a cup of dog food and filled the first dish, then I got a cup for the other one and put that in the dish. What the ... the dish was full of water! Where did that water come from? I checked the dogs' pail and it was full of water. It wasn't possible for any water to get in there. I thought it was a prank or something.

"Then at 9:00 a.m. the next morning I was at the hotel sitting in the pub reading your book *Haunted Ontario*, and occasionally glancing up to watch the Olympics on the television. A guest staying in room 4 came down and inquired if the bar television was connected to the television in his room. I said it wasn't. It's all cable. He said that he was watching CNN when someone or something changed the channels."

When we arrived at the Albion we were warmly greeted by Kim, Shelly Know, the hotel manager, Jack (Kim's dad), and Stella and Betty, (Jack's friends). Jack informed me that Betty was sensitive to spirit activity and wanted to join in the investigation.

The tour of the hotel began in the dining room which was originally the bar where Harvey Elliott had died. Kim said the gun Fred used to kill his brother was found behind the bar.

Betty said, "I feel three spots that give me the chills. I have goosebumps on my arms. The presence is male."

Upstairs there were seven bedsitting rooms. Kim led us into the common room, which had been Kim's bedroom. Shelly Know, who had managed the hotel for the past several years, spoke about the unexplained activity in the building.

"Not many years ago we were hosting the annual golf tournament. We were sitting in this common room folding T-shirts when four books suddenly flew off the bookcase. The employee with me fled downstairs."

Shelly placed the books back on the shelf and went back to the pub. She returned later to discover the same books back on the floor again.

"Another day after closing we were sitting here in the common room when we heard the door at the top of the stairs open and close. We were the only ones in the building. Then we heard footsteps."

One night Shelly and three other employees got the shock of their lives in the pub area. "It was midnight and we were closed. There we were sitting on a bench facing the bar. The Rickard's Red tap suddenly turned on all by itself and started spraying beer all over the bar and onto the floor."

During renovations in 2000, Shelly and an employee named Judy shared an experience upstairs. At the time all the doors on the second floor had been removed. The women were sitting in the office, just off the common room. "We heard the door at the top of the stairs open, but there was no door to open! We called this ghost Molly."

Shelly also told me about a light in the dining room alcove that comes on by itself during the night. Betty confirmed that there was activity in that alcove.

One night during the dinner hour, Lisa Muszynski, Kim's sister, and one of the chefs, were standing behind the bar when they watched two glasses, hanging from the rack, move forward and crash to the floor.

Local historian Reg Thompson offered to share some information with us. Reg is extremely knowledgeable about the history of the area and has personally researched the murder of Harvey Elliott. Does Reg think the Albion Hotel is haunted?

"I really couldn't say. I haven't seen a glass of beer fly off the shelf, but when it's quiet in the evening and only one or two people are in the pub, sometimes we think someone has just come through the front door. We hear it. The conversation stops. No one comes in to the bar and no one goes out either. You never hear anything else."

Kim has a suggestion to make if you want to book a specific room:

"I had a couple staying in room 4. It was late at night. I only had one room booked. At 12:30 a.m. we closed the hotel and left for the night. The next morning our guests came down and asked who was playing the guitar downstairs the previous night. They were surprised that there was no applause after the playing ended. I checked with all the employees but there had been no one in the building at the time.

"A group of friends and I decided to go down the street after closing time. One of the girls in the group was not feeling well. She decided to retire to room 4 until we returned. We got back at 2:30 a.m. The poor girl was terrified. She had heard footsteps going back and forth and back and forth in the hallway. She knew she was the only person in the building."

Mike Parkinson, a chef, had an amazing experience one New Year's Eve.

"After we did the dinner we went up and showered and changed. We were about to come downstairs to join the party. The time was 11:45 p.m. I came out of the room. I opened the door to go downstairs. I saw a figure sitting on the steps facing the front door. No one else was in the area. The woman appeared bulky in the shoulder area. Her brunette hair hung down to her shoulders. Her head was bent down. I let go of the door to get Lisa and then I thought 'who was that?'

"I opened the door again, but she was gone. People were milling around in the front hallway. I looked for her in the crowd but she was nowhere to be seen. Then on New Year's Day when I was there at the hotel doing the inventory, I knew I was not alone in the building."

An interesting cast of characters is in this little village, ghost and otherwise. It is a gorgeous setting and has a wonderful welcome mat. Should you miss this stop? Not a ghost of a chance!

The Royal Ontario Museum

~ Toronto ~

Is the Royal Ontario Museum haunted? If it is, no one at the ROM is talking. Nevertheless, articles have been written about hauntings there. Considering what we already know about the Canadian Museum of Nature in Ottawa - perhaps we should look a little deeper into this one.

Let us begin with what has been written in the past. Bette Shepherd, a ROM volunteer, led a ghost walk in Toronto on April 23, 1980. One of the members of the tour was Wendy Herman, a journalist with the *Toronto Star*, who later wrote an article about the ghost walk. During the walk the group sauntered through the halls of the museum and eventually entered the McLaughlin Planetarium to hear about the ghost of a little girl who has been seen seated in the auditorium. John Robert Colombo, in his book *Haunted Toronto* states, "She was about eight years old. She wore a long white dress and seemed lost among the seats and the stars. She was even sighted when the dome-room was otherwise empty on a number of occasions between 1975 and 1980."

Some people call her Celeste. Her fate has not been traced since the domed theatre closed on November 5, 1995.

No employees at the ROM, when questioned about Celeste, have ever heard of such a story. Although they did acknowledge that there were rumours about hauntings, not one could quote any sources for information. The only alternative, therefore, was to do some research on the background of the museum for myself.

The Royal Ontario Museum is the largest public museum in Canada. In 1851 a provincial museum was established in the Normal and Model Schools, now the site of the Ryerson Polytechnical Institute. Sir Edmund Walker and others petitioned the Legislative Assembly of Ontario, on April 16, 1912, to pass the *ROM Act* which created the Royal Ontario Museum. This institution was made up of five separate museums: Archaeology, Geology, Mineralogy, Paleontology, and Zoology, and each had its own director, administration, and budget. The ROM opened its doors to the public in 1914.

The University of Toronto played a key role in the development of the museum by sharing the operating costs with the government and by turning over some of its teaching collections to the museum. Some faculty members of the university worked as senior staff at the museum.

Charles Trick Currelly was the first director of the Royal Ontario Museum of Archaeology. Mr. Currelly was born in the village of Exeter, Ontario in 1876 and was later educated at Victoria College. Although originally trained as a Methodist minister, Mr. Currelly was drawn to archaeological work in Egypt under the tutelage of the famed Egyptologist Sir Flinders Petrie. He later worked in Crete and Asia Minor.

In 1902 Currelly travelled to Europe with a collection of Roman coins that had been given to him; while there, he took a position as an assistant archaeologist with the British Museum. During his field work with the British Museum he had the opportunity to make purchases and send them back to Victoria College. What was the nature of the objects he collected? Three years later in 1905, he returned to Toronto and, along with others, he persuaded scholars and politicians that the museum they were then planning should belong to the University of Toronto. This request received official sanction and he was appointed to collect artifacts for the new museum. This became a life-long passion — to see the institution grow to become one of the great museums of the world.

Mr. Currelly is now credited with some of the outstanding collections in the Museum, particularly in the Art and Archaeology departments. He retired as Director of Royal Ontario Museum of Archeology in 1946. Or did he?

There are some indications that Charles Trick Currelly may still be walking the exhibitions halls and the corridors of the museum. Some security personnel have reported seeing a "gentleman gowned in a nightshirt." This information would seem to point the finger at Currelly, since he often worked so late in his office that he would choose to spend the night at the museum. He was obviously comfortable among the objects he had uncovered. One wonders what his favourites might have been or which ones have had the greatest impact on him. Perhaps the passage from John Robert Colombo's book tells us something, "He is seen in the Bishop White Gallery which displays the priceless East Asiatic Collection that was gathered in China by William Charles White. Currelly was responsible for the collection coming to the ROM."

The real story of museum hauntings points to the artifacts themselves. As one employee told me, "I don't believe in the stories about the little girl or the ones about Currelly. It is the objects, the artifacts in the museum that possess spiritual energy or power." It immediately reminded me of the sacred objects in the Canadian Museum of Nature in Ottawa. Are we naive to assume that inanimate objects have no life force, no power?

It is common knowledge that the ROM has six million objects in its collections, and I want to investigate their "power." The Ancient Egypt gallery displays Egyptian mummy cases and masks. One coffin, of the court musician Djedmaatesankh (850 B.C.), features spectacular decorations and hieroglyphic inscriptions, all of which are painted in bright colours and adorned with gold leaf. The case is so valuable that the ROM's researchers refuse to risk destroying the stunning designs to inspect the body inside. However, a recent high-tech CAT scan has revealed that the body is adorned with jewellery and that the unfortunate woman died of a severe tooth abscess at the approximate age of 35.

The Bishop White Gallery of Chinese Temple Art features 14 monumental Buddhist sculptures dating from the 12th to the 16th century, as well as three rare Chinese wall paintings circa 1300. Spanning more than 6,000 years of Chinese history, the T. T. Tsui Galleries of

Chinese Art highlights ancient Chinese artifacts including outstanding examples of early weapons, tools, oracle bones used by diviners to predict the future, and animal and mythical figures.

The Nisga'a and Haida Carved Poles stand just beyond the main entrance to the museum. The poles are made from red cedar trees and are covered with huge carvings depicting animals, human spirits, and mythical creatures.

The downstairs section of the building houses a North American Native exhibit. A headdress of eagle feathers that belonged to the legendary Sitting Bull, chief of the Hunkpapa division of the Teton Sioux (Lakota) people is on display. Following the battle of Little Big Horn in 1876, Sitting Bull and his followers sought refuge at Wood Mountain, south of Saskatchewan's Cypress Hills. When he was later promised a pardon by the United States Government, Sitting Bull returned to the United States in 1881. On his departure, he presented his headdress to his friend Major James Morrow Walsh of the Royal Canadian Mounted Police, noting that each of the feathers "marks some deed in war while yet the Sioux were strong."

From the research I have done about Sitting Bull, I know that he had been a bird expert and seemed to identify with them in many ways. He was knowledgeable about birds and about their ways; his speeches were full of references to birds, and he was fond of telling stories about the Bird People. He learned to understand the speech of birds, particularly the Magpie and the Western Meadowlark. Repeatedly, such birds gave him timely warnings. This renders a headdress of this nature to be a very sacred object.

Curious to see what other First Nations items were in storage at the ROM, I requested a copy of the Ontario Archaeological Report of 1897–98, compiled by archaeologist David Boyle (no relation to me). Interesting discoveries were made!

Boyle located a medicine mask used by Chief Ska-na-wa-ti, an Onondaga Fire-keeper and one of the leading Iroquois medicine men on the Grand River Reserve in Ontario. Boyle also found Ska-na-wa-ti's turtle shell rattle, used in certain aspects of a medicine-making ceremony. As Iroquois wampum belt was also on the list. Wampum belts were used by the Iroquois to communicate their laws and agreements. It had been buried along with others during the Colonial war and unearthed by Boyle.

Boyle listed bird amulets and wolf teeth found in a grave in Bexley Township in Victoria County, Ontario. And the list went on! A great many articles in David Boyle's collection were sacred objects. For that matter most items in any collection have something to do with spirituality, symbolism and the sacred. That is partly why they survived intact — protected by their own energy and by those who honoured that energy field. What does this really mean?

We know that symbols communicate or represent ideas, concepts, and feelings which are intangible or invisible. Symbols are alive; they have many levels at which they may be understood and therefore they are not fixed; they can grow with you; they are endowed with a spiritual energy which renders them very sacred, something to be treated with very special care.

Relics that are symbolic, therefore, are a vehicle to express the spirit which might not otherwise be perceived. An awesome responsibility, to care for them!

Have you ever stood in a museum and observed the people milling about the exhibits? It is incredible. There is true magic here. Museum artifacts have power, energy, and an enormous effect on many people. Some visitors are mesmerized by the things they see while others feel totally empowered, some people kneel and pray, some weep, and some people receive messages.

Native people say that the soul of a person is what reaches out to touch the mysterious. Objects that reach out to touch must, by that definition, have souls. This makes a museum a house of souls, a collection of haunting artifacts that touch those who are open to them. It makes a museum a place where people can connect to visions and dreams, a place to be with objects that take them beyond the everyday world. Have you ever recalled how time just seemed to fly by you during a museum visit? Where did the time go and where did you go?

A museum is clearly a place of mysteries and of the unexpected. It is a place that can haunt you. A different kind of haunting.

The great scholar Northrop Frye once recalled, "Dr. Currelly had the extraordinary knack of persuading people, including children, to look with their own eyes, and with their eyes bring the dreamlike pageants of history and geography to life." He was in essence asking people to look at an object and connect the soul, to dream and to see. Currelly knew the power of the objects. Does he haunt the museum? Did he furnish the place with things to haunt the museum? Or does he remain there to tend them still?

Acknowledgements

I WOULD LIKE TO THANK THE FOLLOWING PEOPLE FOR THEIR KIND assistance: Nancy Audet, Niki Bainbridge, Tiffany and Ken Bol, Curt and Kaaren Brandt, Debbie Burton, Joanne Chiusolo, Lorraine and Sam Chiusolo, Scotty Chiusolo, Eleanor Fielding, Ruth Hughes, Yvonne and Ernie Hunt, Jack Hutton, Janine at Merrifield's Bookstore in Woodstock, Allene Kane, Margaret and Wayne McGibney, Cathy Morrow, Chris and Pat Raible, Sylvia and Arthur Rickard, Norman and Rosalie Rondeau, Linda and Robert Salts and Glen Shackleton.

If You would like to Visit

The Albion Hotel
P.O. Box 114
Bayfield, Ontario
NOM 1GO
519-565-2641

Algonquin Provincial Park
Whitney, Ontario
705-633-5572
www.algonquinpark.on.ca

The Bala Bay Inn
P.O. Box 257
Bala, Ontario POC 1AO
705-762-3314

Canadian Museum of Nature
P.O. Box 3443, Station D
Ottawa, Ontario K1P 6P4
613-566-4730
www.nature.ca

Donnelly Homestead
34937 Roman Line, R.R. #3
Lucan, Ontario N0M 2J0
519-227-1244
http://home.quadro.net/~donnelly
rsalts@quadro.net

Jester's Court
279 Queen Street
Port Perry, Ontario L9L 1B9
905-985-2775
www.jesterscourt.ca

Inn at the Falls
P.O. Box 1139
1 Dominion Street
Bracebridge, Ontario P1L 1V3
705-645-2245
Innatthefalls.net

Ottawa Jail Hostel
75 Nicholas Street
Ottawa, Ontario K1N 7B9
613-235-2595

The Mackenzie Inn
P.O. Box 255
Kirkfield, Ontario KOM 2BO
705-438-1278
www.themackenzieinn.com/

Prince George Hotel
200 Ontario Street
Kingston, Ontario K7L 2Y9
613-547-9037

The Severn River Inn
(Inn is currently closed.)
1002 Cowbell Lane
Severn Bridge, Ontario POE 1NO
705-689-6333

Bibliography

Books

Addison, Ottelyn. *Tom Thomson, the Algonquin Years*. Toronto: McGraw-Hill Ryerson, 1969.

Angus, James T. *Severn River*. Orillia: Severn Publications Ltd, 1995.

Beck, Peggy V & Walters, A.L. *The Sacred*. Tsaile: Navajo Community College, 1980.

Blodwen, Davies. *Paddle and Palette*. Toronto: Ryerson Press, 1930.

Boyer, Victoria. *Memories of Bracebridge*. Bracebridge: Herald-Gazette Press, 1975.

Boyle, Terry. *Under This Roof*. Toronto: Doubleday Canada, 1980.

Boyle, Terry. *Haunted Ontario 2*. Toronto: Polar Bear Press, 1999.

Boyle, Terry. *Marilyn At French River*. Toronto: Polar Bear Press, 2003.

Burks, Eddie & Cribbs. Gillian. *Ghosthunter*. Headline Book Publishing, 1995.

Cochrane, Hugh. *Gateway to Oblivion*. New York: Doubleday, 1980.

Columbo, John Robert. *Haunted Toronto*. Toronto: Hounslow Press, 1996.

Davis, Carole. *The Skull Speaks*. Toronto: Amhrea Publishing, 1985.

Farmer, Samuel. *On the Shores of Scugog*. Port Perry: The Port Perry Star Press, 1934.

Fazakas, Ray. *The Donnelly Album*. Willowdale: Firefly Books, 1995.

Fleming R.B. *The Railway King of Canada*. Vancouver: UBC Press, 1991.

Fletcher, Katharine. *Capital Walks*. Toronto: McClelland & Stewart Ltd., 1993.

Hoffman, Elizabeth P. *In Search of Ghosts*. Philadelphia: Camino Books, Inc., 1992.

Lidgold, Carole. *The History of the Guild Inn*. Toronto: Brookridge Publishing House, 2000.

Little,William T. *The Tom Thomson Mystery*. Toronto: McGraw Hill, 1970.

Mika, Helma & Nick. *Places in Ontario*. Belleville: Mika Publishing, 1983.

Royal Ontario Museum. *Worlds to Explore*. Toronto: Royal Ontario Museum, 1997.

Salts, J. Robert. *You are Never Alone*. Lucan: published by James Robert Salts, 1996.

Saunders, Audrey. *The Algonquin Story*. Toronto: Ontario Department of Land and Forests, 1946.

Spell, Sarah C. *The Hermitage*. Clarke A. Wilcox, 1973.

Symons, Doug M. *The Village that Straddled a Swamp*. Woodstock:The Oxford Historical Society, 1997.

Upton, Kyle. *Niagara's Ghosts at Fort George*. Newmarket: K. Upton, 1999.

Vestal, Stanley. *Sitting Bull*. Norman: University of Oklahoma Press, 1989.

Newspapers

Bennet, Michael, *The Hamilton Spectator*, "The Hauntings of Halton," 1987.

"Ferguson Norman," *The Muskoka Sun*, Thursday, June 16, 1983.

Fragomeni, Carmela. "Halloween Busy for Canada's Top Ghost Hunter," *The Hamilton Spectator*, October 31, 2001.

"Ghost Road," *The Port Perry Star*, Tuesday, October 30, 1990.

"Ghost Story," *The Port Perry Star*, Tuesday, July 26, 1983. *The Goderich Signal*, November 11, 1987.

"Holiday House," *The Herald Gazette*, Thursday, January 22, 1976.

Huron Expositor, February, 20, 1880.

Hutton, Jack, *The Muskoka Sun*, Thursday, August 11, 1983.

Hutton, Jack, *The Muskoka Sun*, Thursday, October 4, 1990.

"James H. Jackson's Severn River Inn," *The Muskoka Sun*, Thursday, October 2, 1997.

Kuzyk, Ron, "Burlington Hotbed of Supernatural Phenomenon," *The Burlington Post*, March 2000.MacLeod, Ian, "The Ghost Road." *The Port Perry Star*, Wednesday, December 28, 1988.

"Manor Makeover," *Century Home*, August 1994.

"New Owners Rekindle Spirit of Mackenzie," *The Lake Simcoe Visitor*, Tuesday, August 24, 1993.

"Obituary Section," *The Parry Sound Star*, May 30, 1968.

Rimstead, Diane, *The Muskoka Sun*, Thursday, October 9, 1997.

"Scugog Road," *The Port Perry Star*, Tuesday, August 23, 1983.

"Severn River Inn," *The Muskoka Sun*, Thursday, August 14, 1997.

Shackleton, Glen, *The Kingston Downtowner*, May–October 1998.

"Woodstock Courthouse," *The Ingersoll Chronicle*, Friday, December 19, 1862.

Plays

Nyquist, Stina, *The Shantyman's Daughter*, Huntsville, 1978.

Magazines

Cruickshank, Tom, "The Best of Bayfield," *Century Home*, June/July 1992.

Deemeester, Meaghan, "Canoe Lake's Voice," *Muskoka Magazine*, May 2006.

Photo Credits

Index